Peter Shen's Face Fortunes

Peter Shen's Face Fortunes

Peter Shen
with Joyce Wilson

Illustrated by Peter Shen

A Perigee Book

Perigee Books
are published by
G.P. Putnam's Sons
200 Madison Avenue
New York, New York 10016

Library of Congress Cataloging in Publication Data

Shen, Peter
  Peter Shen's Face fortunes.

  "A Perigee book."
  1. Physiognomy. I. Wilson, Joyce, Joint Author. II. Title.
BF1891.F5S53 1982   138   81-8531
ISBN 0-399-12669-4   AACR2
ISBN 0-399-50585-7 (pbk.)

First Perigee Printing, 1982
Printed in the United States of America

To my Parents—Clara and H. K. Shen

ACKNOWLEDGMENTS

Our thanks go to our editor, Judy Linden, whose unfailing charm, enthusiasm and perspicacity cheered us on; to Iris Bass, our designer; to Judith A. Thompson, who engineered the typescript; and to all others who contributed to the production of this book.

CONTENTS

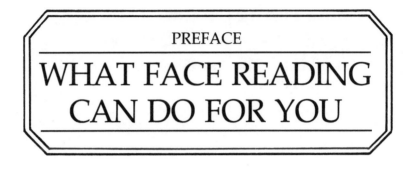

WHAT FACE READING CAN DO FOR YOU

Here is a fascinating way to gain new insight into yourself and others and become a more interesting person. Don't be put off because there seems to be a lot to explore. With this book you'll learn how to:

- gain quick insight into the compatibility of a lover, co-worker or friend
- discover your potential for success in business, work, personal relationships and other areas of achievement
- stage your life plan, year by year, for a successful outcome to any enterprise
- compensate for any limitation and make the most of your assets
- make a better impression and learn what others are saying to you through their face and features
- identify the major characteristics that produce wealth, success, health, vitality, longevity and satisfactory life relationships

Do you have a nose for money? Eyebrows for fame? A jaw for status? Cheekbones for power?

What are the signs of an ideal husband? A perfect wife? What are your prospects for travel, romance, security?

These are only a few of the questions face reading can answer—while providing you with a whole new dimension for appreciation of yourself and others.

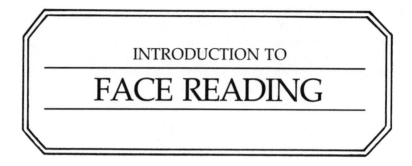

INTRODUCTION TO

FACE READING

The ancient Chinese art of face reading has as much meaning for people today as it had in the past. The origins of Chinese face reading are lost in antiquity. Yet it is believed that it was the source of or had a common source with other prescientific methods of divination. The art was recorded as long ago as the time of Confucius in the sixth and fifth centuries B.C., during the Spring and Autumn period of Chinese culture. Since then, various systems of face reading have developed. Here we follow the Teaching of the Linen Robe, one of many schools no longer attached to any particular sect but still practiced by professional face readers in China and around the world.

Chinese face reading shares with other teachings the principle of "as above, so below." This means that earth reflects the state of the cosmos. In Chinese face reading, the order of the Celestial Sphere (the cosmos) was said to be reflected in the order of the Chinese Imperial Court, and the order of the court was reflected in the face of any individual. So any nuance in the nature of an individual and any event in the life of that person is discernible in face reading.

Face reading is, in a sense, prescientific. But today's science from time to time confirms some of the indications of the early teachings. Lines in the hand, whorls in the fingerprints, certain markings on the ears, and characteristics of the features are suggestive of heart and brain problems and so relate personality to physical characteristics. Today's science also tends to be deterministic. We are born with certain genes that determine our characteristics—in a sense, our destiny.

In face reading, aptitudes, personality traits and potentialities are, indeed, shown in the features and other facial markings. They are assumed to be inborn and in that sense are also predetermined. Yet no feature is good or bad per se. The question to be asked is "Good for what?" The nose, for example, represents wealth, but just as the display of wealth takes different forms, the shape of the nose can show the potential for generosity, extravagance, thrift, miserliness or accumulation. The key here is to know your own strengths and weaknesses, predelictions and potentials (and those of others with whom you live or work). First, know yourself. Then make an effort to display your positive characteristics and conceal your negative ones. You are not doomed by any feature; you are only guided to your strengths and weaknesses, so you know what you need to compensate for and what you can rely on.

Life-style affects features, and you can control your appearance and how your face develops so that you assume a harmony and glow. For example, a mouth that is slack and turned down at the corners is often a result of discontent and failure to realize the potential offered by other features; it can, instead, through "inner rightness," become a firm, confident mouth promising integrity in later years. Also, crinkles at the corners of the eyes indicate frivolous sexuality and are put there by the constant narrowing and widening of the eyes of one who is, in fact, subservient, ever out to please.

In Chinese face reading, when the heart is straight, the face will glow and the features will appear in harmony. Rightness of heart can create a glow that brings any face into harmony. It also explains how we create our own features—shape the mouth, put lines beside the eyes, firm or slacken the chin through behavior and life-style.

In working with this book, you can move about, picking out areas in which you can have the immediate reward of knowing your fortune of the moment; or you can proceed step by step, increasing your knowledge of every aspect of face reading. Face reading ordinarily proceeds according to eight basic steps.

1. Look at the five elements. What type (Fire, Earth, Water, Wood, Gold) or mixed type is this individual?
2. Evaluate the cosmic energies (active Yang, receptive Yin) as reflected in the face.
3. Evaluate the Three Stations—the lengthwise divisions of the face. Are they balanced or is there an unusual situation?
4. Judge the features of the face—the mountains (prominent features) and rivers (moisture-producing features). Also individually evaluate the Five Major Features, the Seven Minor Features and the lesser features of the face for their indications.
5. Listen to the voice and observe the posture, how the head is held.
6. Are the colors (planetary colors) appropriate to the features?
7. Look at the position point, the designated area for the current year of age. For a life reading, examine the 13 Middle Points.
8. Discern whether the individual has warmth, heart and inner glow.

For the outcome of enterprises the individual is currently engaged in or contemplating, look at the appropriate palace or palaces and also (for achievement) at the Star Points.

PART ONE

THE FACE
AT FIRST GLANCE

When we encounter another person for the first time, the face we see is not the face we are going to get to know in five minutes, five days, even five years—however long we'll have that face before us.

The first impact is of the *persona,* the idea of self that the other person projects. Eyes meet. An exchange of energy takes place. We speak, or we do not speak. But an image of that other self has sunk into our psyche. The encounter may be brief. We may quickly forget it. But the image is there. It can be called up by hypnosis. It may appear in our dreams or in hypnogogic sleep. Or the other self may become a part of our life pattern. This may become a familiar face. Even so, you may not really see it, even if you catch it in a moment of repose. You may never really see the face till some moment of crisis or endearment suddenly brings you to see the person as he or she really is. This may distress or enchant you. How many of us have said: "I never imagined what he (she) was really like until . . ."

But what he or she is really like is there—written in the face for you to read even at first glance. How much better off all of us would be if we could separate the fantasy from the reality in our relationships instead of having to wait for that moment of truth.

This is not to suggest that you stand back and study another person before you make eye contact or speak or otherwise acknowledge your meeting. Or that you should never get caught up in the glamour of personality or try to crack the shell of every recluse you get stonewalled by. The masquerade is part of us all.

Nevertheless, by becoming familiar with the personality pointers apparent in the face, you can tune into their message and separate the reality from the mask and be competent to handle both. You can better enjoy a relationship as a result.

You can also become at ease with your own face. Knowing your assets and potentialities liberates your charm. Your weak spots need not be sore spots—recognized, they will cease to dominate you. Everyone has at least one fortunate feature; no one is perfect. The greatest charm is to accept yourself.

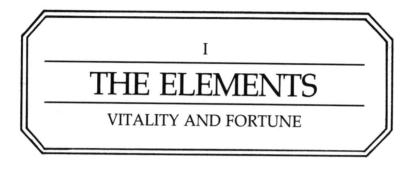

I

THE ELEMENTS

VITALITY AND FORTUNE

The ancient Chinese watched the sky and knew five plan-ets—Mars, Mercury, Saturn, Venus and Jupiter. In China, each planet was associated with a particular element for which it was named:

Mars:	Fire Star
Mercury:	Water Star
Saturn:	Earth Star
Venus:	Gold Star
Jupiter:	Wood Star

These planetary elements are each represented by a particular color, vitality (form of energy) and fortune, or lot in life:

Planetary Element	Color	Vitality	Fortune
Fire	red	activity	adventure
Water	black	flexibility	wealth
Earth	brown	stillness	security
Gold	white	grace	status
Wood	green	rising	wisdom

Out of this developed the cluster of personality traits linked in face reading to the face shapes and complexion color.

Face Shapes

We begin face reading by looking, again, at the elements. Each is associated with a particular face shape, complexion color, personality type and vocational field. Note that these are *pure* elemental face shapes:

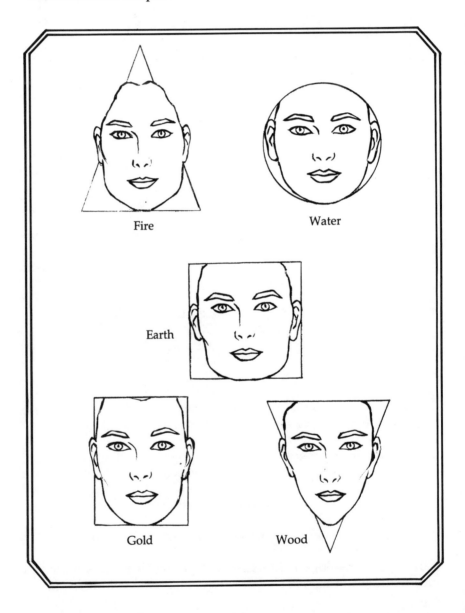

Fire

Water

Earth

Gold

Wood

There are also three common mixed elemental face shapes:

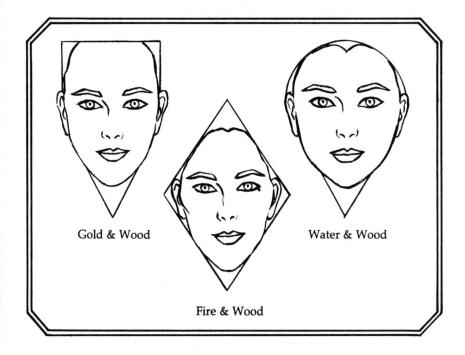

Gold & Wood

Fire & Wood

Water & Wood

However, *any* elemental face type may show signs, usually complexion color, of carrying another element (for example, a Fire type with pale skin). So there are a variety of combinations—twenty-five in all.

In combination, elements may help or hinder one another:

Water helps Wood	Earth hinders Water
Wood helps Fire	Water hinders Fire
Fire helps Earth	Fire hinders Gold
Earth helps Gold	Gold hinders Wood
Gold helps Water	Wood hinders Earth

For example, a fire-shape (conic) face is naturally ruddy but is helped by olive coloring (Wood) and is weakened by swarthiness (Water). However, one should not be too judgmental about this. A little Gold (pallor), for example, may not weaken Wood if the person is sturdy; he or she may just be a late bloomer.

What you can learn right away about yourself or another from the elements is this: All pure types (with color appropriate to face shape) are effective people. All mixed types are either positive or stressful, depending on the beneficial or detracting effect of the combined elements and the degree to which the weakening element is present. If you analyze your own elements, you can often tell at a glance whether another person will be compatible or hindering to your own vitality. In choosing a partner, it is wise not to choose someone of your own element. Rather, choose one who will be benefiting—meaning, giving you a better life.

1. THE COLORFUL FIRE PEOPLE

Planet: Mars. Element: Fire. Color: red. Vitality: activity. Fortune: adventure. Face Shape: conic. Complexion: ruddy. Helped by Wood; helps Earth; hinders Gold; hindered by Water.

Fire rises upward in points—like the flame of a candle or a wood fire on a hearth. Fire is restless in movement, changeable in form. It glows with a reddish-orangish flame. It gives warmth, but it may also be destructive.

The Fire Face. The Fire face, like its element, rises from a broad base—the jawline—narrowing toward a point at the forehead. Usually the pure Fire person has sharp, pointed features—very sharp cheekbones, for example—and all the bones in the face seem to show. The complexion is ruddy; the hair is curly and usually a bright color,; there are gold flecks in the eyes; the skin appears dry. Look, too, at the hands. The Fire person's hands are thin and bony, and the fingers are pointed. The body is wiry.

The Fire Personality. The Fire personality is outgoing, exciting, temperamental, restless. He or she is magnetic, strong-minded; there is never a dull moment in this person's company. Fire people are extroverts, outdoorsy, interested in sports, always busy, doing things. Because they are people oriented, they make friends easily, are easy to talk to and will usually have interesting things to report—and will probably be first to start a conversation.

Fire Vitality. Fire people like to move from place to place, never staying long anywhere. Their Vitality is activity.

Fire Fortune. The Fire fortune is adventure. Fire people lead a colorful life. They are actors and actresses, reporters, publicists, salespersons, politicians. They know everybody. They find success in dealing with people, being in the public eye. They enjoy applause.

Fire Combinations

- If the Fire face has an olive (grayish-green) complexion, it means that he or she is carrying Wood, and that is beneficial. Such people often succeed in life at an early age—often in theater, politics, the military.
- If the face is pale, it means the Fire person is carrying Gold, and as Fire hinders Gold, it suggests the person may be a status-seeker or overly ambitious but does not succeed.
- If the angles of the Fire face are squared and the complexion is tawny, it indicates that he or she is carrying Earth. As Fire helps Earth, this individual may have more stability and security than a pure Fire type.
- If the Fire face is swarthy, particularly if it is fleshy or rounded and the head is large, the Fire person is carrying Water, which hinders Fire. Even though the person may be superintelligent or talented, this person may have difficulty expressing his personality or may have his talents dimmed or become eccentric. Then it is wise to seek some indications of Wood in the physical structure, as Wood helps Fire and Water helps Wood. A tall, bony figure, for example, would be an indication that there is some basic wisdom and high-mindedness in the personality to help overcome any difficulties.

Fire People Pairups

- A Fire person benefits when he or she pairs with Wood. Wood's Vitality is rising, so they can move upward together; Wood's Fortune is sagacity, wisdom, which the Fire personality often lacks and so finds helpful for success. A Wood person may, however, find a Fire personality unstable and superficial.
- The Fire personality is beneficial to an Earth personality when they pair up together. This is because the Fire person brings some action to Earth's stillness and shakes

up Earth's security so the earthling's life doesn't become too dull. The Fire partner, however, may get restless and become bored by Earth's stability.

- A Fire person and a Water person make a stressful combination. Water puts out the Fire—though Water's tendency to accumulate wealth tempts the Fire personality. A Fire person may borrow or cadge or attempt to relieve the Water person of money in some other way. Water's flexibility combined with Fire's activity can be very unstable. The combination creates steam.
- The effect of Fire on Gold is to melt it. Under this influence, Gold loses its grace—and its high status is threatened, although Gold may attract, by its position in life, the restless active Fire.

Are You a Fire Personality?

Fire (pure type): positive. Conic face, ruddy complexion. Thin, straight, wiry frame. You are very fortunate. Pair with Wood for support. Avoid Water.

Fire-Wood (mixed type): positive. Conic face with olive complexion or diamond-shape face with olive or ruddy complexion. Receptive. You are fortunate, but perhaps too knowing to take the chances that lead to the peak of success. Pair with Wood or Wood-Fire.

Fire-Earth (mixed type): neutral. Conic face with sallow complexion; square jawed. Supportive. Moderately fortunate. Will have security if not high success. Pair with Earth or with Earth-Fire.

Fire-Gold (mixed type): stressful. Conic face with pale complexion. Charming and adaptable but lacking in purpose to achieve success. Pair with Wood or Earth for spiritual support or more stability.

Fire-Water (mixed type): stressful. Conic face with swarthy complexion or fleshy face. Restless movement without purpose. Tends to be ineffectual, wastes effort. Pair with Wood for guidance and uplift, for Wood is compatible with both your elements.

2. THE WEALTHY WATER PEOPLE

Planet: Mercury. Element: Water. Color: black. Vitality: flexibility. Fortune: wealth. Face shape: round. Complexion: swarthy. Helped by Gold; helps Wood; hinders Fire; hindered by Earth.

Water flows into pools; it falls as raindrops; it is stored in wells. Everything about water is round, fluid. Its color is black—like the darkness of a well or a mountain lake. Its Vitality is flexibility, for it takes the shape of whatever is holding it. Its Fortune is wealth—water makes life possible and rich. The waters of the earth teem with life. Water accumulates; it can be collected and stored. It falls from the sky and springs from the earth. It helps Wood by making growth possible. It is helped by Gold, which brings grace. It is hindered by Earth, which makes it muddy. It diminishes Fire by extinguishing it.

The Water Face. The Water face is round and may be fleshy; bones do not show. Lips are mobile or loose and eyes tend to protrude. Usually ears, eyes, mouth and nose are also rounded in shape. Hands are fleshy and soft and the bones don't show; the fingers are thick and rounded. Even the figure is rounded in the pure Water type, with the back shaped somewhat like a turtle's shell. In the pure Water type, the skin is swarthy and appears moist. A Water type may sweat profusely. The mouth is full and moist. The eyes are dark and dewy and often have a lot of white showing around the iris.

The Water Personality. The Water personality adapts to any situation and comes out wealthier. Water people are clear-headed, bright, interesting, witty conversationalists and diplomatic (as indicated by showing no bones). They are smart business people, good in management. Their adaptability makes them seemingly responsive to everyone else, so they can circulate freely among all types and find ready acceptance.

The Water Vitality. Water is flexible. It fills any available space, but it cannot be compressed. It will rise and fall in flood or drought. Water also changes form with the temperature—from ice to fluid to vapor. This means that Water people are always ready to fill the space available to them and change their form as the situation may require.

Water Fortune. The Fortune of the Water personality is wealth.

Water people are likely to be business people or financiers (if the pure type). Their assets are liquid, so they are always prepared to make a profitable investment. They are attracted to fluid transactions, like the stock exchange, banking, money funds—and always have an eye out (full eyes) for a lucrative deal. For all the Water type's diplomacy and charm, he or she is really interested in accumulating wealth and tends to be an opportunist, wondering (while he or she charms you) how you can be used to an advantage. Enjoy the Water person, but remember there is no such thing as a free lunch.

Water Combinations

- The Water person obviously benefits when carrying Gold. A pale complexion (with a round face) adds grace to the Water personality and raises the status, the heights that can be reached socially or in business or a profession.
- If the Water type has an olive complexion, the Water person is carrying Wood. Water benefits Wood—helps it grow—and the lofty-minded, idealistic, sagacious influence of Wood can elevate the Water personality.
- If the face is ruddy, the Water personality is carrying Fire. Any Gold (refinement, grace) in the Water type will be negated by this combination; and as Water negates Fire, the charm and restless activity of this element may create a dilettante—one who dabbles but does not really achieve the wealth that is deserved.
- With a tawny skin (Earth), the Water personality's charm may be muddied and the flexibility hampered. He or she may seek a security that is out of keeping with the necessary fluidity of this element, and consequently suffer losses rather than gains.

Water People Pairups

- Gold is obviously the perfect choice for the Water personality. The classic example of this is the self-made financier who marries a socialite and raises his status along with, probably, the opportunity to make even more money. Gold (grace, status) helps Water (wealth).
- Conversely, Water (wealth, flexibility) can help the high-minded intellectual Wood (rising, wisdom). A classic example of this is the creative artist or scientist of either

sex who marries a rich Water spouse, who supports the creative person during the period of development and allows the other to grow. Often the man or woman seriously engaged in making money has a spiritually or artistically oriented spouse. Water helps Wood, but it is not totally unrewarded. Wood brings added values to the Water person's life—and because this element is emotional as well as smart about money, it also benefits from the relationship with Wood.

- Water and Fire, as we have seen, is not a fortunate combination. Fire is too restless, too eager to be in the public eye, to put up for long with Water's diplomatic, docile circulation and will always feel dampened in the relationship. Somehow an arrangement might be worked out, but it would not be an easy one.
- Water and Earth is another difficult pairing. Earth, because of its need for security and its very stability, blocks the circulation of Water, binds it in the earth as ground water, stilling it. True, Earth helps Gold, which in turn is helpful to Water, but someone so bound to stability and solidity is not likely to be supportive to the flexible Water personality.
- Water and Water is another hazardous combination. You should not pair with your own element, and although it is said that money attracts money, it is better to pair with someone who contributes to your success, who is supportive, rather than to join with one who has the same goals. With Water, this is particularly true, for an excess of Water creates flooding, and this can be destructive.

Are You a Water Personality?

Water (pure type): positive. Round face, swarthy complexion. You are very fortunate and destined for success. Pair with Gold.

Water-Gold (mixed type): positive. Round face, ivory complexion. You are fortunate and have the wisdom to control your acquisitiveness. Pair with Gold-Water.

Water-Wood (mixed type): positive. Round face, olive complexion. You may be too idealistic to completely realize your financial goals, but you are likely to be philanthropic, which is beneficial to others. Pair with Wood or Wood-Water.

Water-Fire (mixed type): inharmonious. Round face, reddish complexion. You have money to burn and you will burn it. Your lust for money can negate your interest in people, and your restless activity can detract from any Gold (grace) in your nature. Pair with Wood, which Water helps and which helps Fire.

Water-Earth (mixed type): stressful. Round face, tawny complexion. Your need for security can bind your flexibility; you make mistakes on the side of security and lose out. Earth hinders your Water element. Pair with Gold, helpful to Water, helped by Earth.

3. THE STABLE EARTH PEOPLE

Planet: Saturn. Element: Earth. Color: yellowish brown. Vitality: stillness. Fortune: security. Face shape: square. Complexion: tawny. Helped by Fire; helps Gold; hindered by Wood; detracts from Water.

Earth is still, solid, stable, and in cosmic geometry, it is represented by the square. Fields are marked off into squares; so are cities—in building lots. The color of Earth—its soil—is brown or yellowish brown. Its Vitality is stillness; its Fortune, security.

The Earth Face. The face shape that represents the element Earth is also square. Its color is tawny—golden tan. Its overall shape and features appear thick and solid. Usually the Earth person is a stocky individual with heavy bones. The hands are square, with thick, blunt fingers. The whole head is square, with the top of the head flat. The Earth person has large features—large ears, large mouth, a prominent nose—a thick waist and a thick back. The face and body are usually well muscled and do not show too much bone but often have prominent veins.

The Earth Personality. The Earth person is aggressive, a doer, solid, big boned. Earth people show stubbornness and willpower; they are set in their minds and can refuse to budge. They tend to stay in one place, needing a secure home and a place to call their own. The need for security can make them more aggressive, and they will defend what is theirs. Do not think these people are dull because they are heavy or that they are not bright because they think more slowly or take longer to make up their minds. They think in terms of power, strength and holding any ground they have won. Once they make decisions, they back them up—and usually their decisions are correct. At least they make them stick.

Earth Vitality. Earth is quiet, unmoving. It spreads about us, unchanging. The Vitality of Earth is stillness. So the Earth person tends to stay put, to stand still, to be patient, to hold his or her ground. The Earth is stable. Rarely does it buffet us about as does Water. It can be trusted. It holds us to it. People settle on it, build homes on it. So, too, Earth people are stable. Their word is their bond.

Earth Fortune. The Fortune of Earth people is security. The prototype of the pure Earth type is the industrialist, the empire builder, the one who expands power from a center out. Those less powerful want a steady income, a steady job and a home of their own.

Earth Combinations

- When the square Earth person has a ruddy face and features that are smaller and sharper, it shows that Earth is carrying Fire. The Earth-Fire person has more activity, more sense of showmanship than pure Earth. But he or she may not be as effective, although Fire, by its upward pointing and restlessness, helps Earth be less of a stick-in-the-mud. Earth-Fire will be more adventurous and more willing to take chances and may be more in the public eye, less hidden behind the scenes than true Earth.
- As Fire helps Earth, Earth helps Gold. The pale-face earthling with a square face will be carrying Gold. This individual is more graceful and more charming and reaches a higher social status than pure Earth, perhaps because Earth-Gold's industry supports a desire for the finer things of life. But it may diminish physical strength and endurance.
- If the Earth personality is carrying Water, it shows up in a certain flabbiness of face and body and a swarthier skin tone. The nose may be more rounded and less prominent with Water. The Earth-Water type may be more interested in money-grubbing, but this does not help a natural urge for security—it may only cause the person to be somewhat miserly, for Earth detracts from Water.
- The Earth personality who is tall and bony and whose skin is olive is probably carrying Wood. Earth-Wood may be more intellectual, more of an esthete than Earth

otherwise is, but these qualities hinder the ability to grasp and hold power and so make this person less effective.

Earth People Pairups

- Earth often marries Earth, because familiarity makes each feel secure. Such a relationship, though, can be heavy and dull. Earth needs the stimulation of Fire, though this is truly a case in which opposites must attract. It works well in a business arrangement where the active Fire is the outside person and the stable Earth works behind the scenes. In marriage, though, the restless Fire may soon tire of Earth and soar upward with a more compatible Wood. However, if Earth can capture a Fire person, Earth will be considerably helped by the alliance.
- Earth will be wonderfully supportive to the graceful, aristocratic Gold, and may indeed find a champion in this relationship, even though the Gold partner feels they have little in common. Gold will, however, be attracted by Earth's leadership and power—and also by the security this element offers.
- Earth should be very cautious about pairing with the idealistic Wood. Basically, Wood represents the high-minded "druid" who is battling the very power the Earth personality depends on for security. It is the ecologist against the industrial plant or the strip miner, and neither will ever understand the other's point of view.
- Earth hinders Water, so Water may suffer more from this partnership. Earth may profit from the wealth Water brings to the relationship, while remaining indifferent to the emotional needs of diplomatic, flexible Water.

Are You an Earth Personality?

Earth (pure type): positive. Square face, tawny coloring. Thick body, strongly muscled. Stable. You are extremely fortunate and effective. Pair with Fire; avoid Wood.

Earth-Fire (mixed type): positive. Square face, ruddy coloring. This is a fortunate combination and very helpful to you. Pair with Fire or Fire-Earth. Avoid Wood and Water.

Earth-Gold (mixed type): neutral. Square face, pale complexion. This is a reasonably fortunate combination. Pair with Gold-

Earth for compatibility; avoid Wood and Fire.

Earth-Water (mixed type): inharmonious. Square face, but flabby. Dark coloring. You tend to be self-defeating, so pair with Gold or Gold-Earth, which helps Water and to which you can be supportive. Avoid Wood, Fire and Water.

Earth-Wood (mixed type): inharmonious. Square, bony face; olive skin. You are less sturdy than other Earth types and may feel your energy is being sapped by your intellect, creating a kind of neurasthenia; unlike most Earth people, you may be physically weak. Pair with a Fire type to gain added strength from the Wood part of your nature and to have your Earth part strengthened. Avoid Gold, Wood and Water.

4. THE ELEGANT GOLD PEOPLE

Planet: Venus. Element: Gold. Color: white. Vitality: grace. Fortune: status. Face shape: oblong. Complexion: ivory. Helped by Earth; helps Water; hinders Wood; hindered by Fire.

Gold (Metal) represents the beautiful planet Venus, which in all cultures is a symbol of beauty and delight. And anyone who has seen this planet as the Evening Star or Morning Star will probably understand the reason. Large, luminous (the brightest object in the night sky other than the moon), Venus floats above the horizon among the beautiful colors of sunrise or sunset and has the magical effect of a rainbow or a spring flower. The Chinese associate this planet with the color white (actually a mixture of light of all colors) and the most precious of metals, gold. Its Vitality is grace, associated with the objects of beauty into which Gold can be transformed, as it is a malleable metal and easy to work into delicate forms. It is also, like the planet, the most gleaming and bright of metals. The Fortune of Gold is to belong to the elite.

The Gold Face. All these qualities are apparent in the Gold face. This is the oblong face, which the Chinese considered the perfect balance in face shapes—each third of the face is of equal length and about the same width, though narrower than it is wide, similar to the ancient Greeks' golden proportion. The true Gold personality has beautiful, luminous eyes, nicely shaped ears, a shapely waist and a slightly rounded abdomen. The hands are graceful and soft, the fingers, smooth and tapering. The top of the head is rounded. The whole look is one of elegant softness, and Gold people carry themselves well, for their Vitality is grace. The color of Gold is white and the Gold complexion color is ivory.

The Gold Personality. The Gold person is elegant and very attractive-looking. They have grace and charm; they are image makers. Usually they are fortunate and come into high positions—as executives, bank managers, higher levels of any kind of employment. Fashion models are often Gold personalities. Gold people are interested in the arts and foster or work at them. Because of their charm, they are usually socially adept and pleasant hosts and hostesses.

Gold Vitality. The Vitality of Gold people is grace. Whatever they do has delicacy and charm. They pave a path of gold with good manners and thus avoid many of the unpleasant confrontations and dismays with which others have to deal. They win others over with their ease and thus smooth their own course.

Gold Fortune. The Fortune of Gold is status. Gold people are born into or rise to the ranks of the elite and thus enjoy the good things of life with little effort. They achieve high social standing. They are the leaders—the image makers—and are admired and often envied. But before you who are not pure Gold envy them too much, appreciate what Confucius had to say about grace: It is beautiful, but it may lack strength.

Gold Combinations

- Gold is helped if it is carrying some of the sturdy Earth element (oblong face with tawny skin). Gold alone may be too soft, too malleable, and needs the security and stability the Earth element provides.
- Gold carrying Water (oblong face and swarthy complexion) benefits from Water's wealth, diplomacy and flexibility which support Gold's grace.
- Gold carrying Fire—oblong face, complexion ruddy—is not so fortunate, for Fire hinders Gold. However, if the Gold person is strong and sturdy in physique (some Earth), a little Fire may be helpful. It is activating without melting the Gold.
- The Gold person carrying some Wood (oval face, tapered chin, with fair complexion) is physically attractive, usu-

ally a favorite child. This person may have high potential but lacks power to carry out projects. This is the face of beauty—but it may lead to one's being a show-off, self-centered, vain, with no true control; and the small chin often shows weakness in later life. The better qualities of Wood—high-mindedness, wisdom—are hindered in the Gold personality.

Gold People Pairups

Should Gold people marry each other? It often happens, because they belong to the superfortunates and are thrown together. They frequently divorce each other, too. Too much grace and high status can lack strength.

- Gold does much better to pair with the solid Earth, who provides the earthy realism and strength this element needs; literature and gossip columns are well spiced with such pairings—the socialite who marries the chauffeur, the industrialist who marries for a rise in society. Gold needs strength, and Earth provides it.
- Gold helps the diplomatic and wealthy Water, and probably is helped by the money that comes with such a pairing. Water has charm as well as money, and this makes a well-matched pair, even if Water benefits more than Gold from the alliance.
- Gold and Fire is not so fortunate a pairing. Fire, as we have seen, melts Gold and further weakens it. Though Fire by its restlessness and upward pointing may temporarily attract or charm Gold, no lasting relationship can form. Fire, however, makes an attractive guest at Gold's parties.
- Gold and Wood do not make a particularly fortunate combination. Wood is too high-minded, too up in the air to be an asset to Gold. And Wood's soaring vitality takes it away from Gold's sphere. Wood's wisdom may be jarred by Gold's dilettantism, while Gold always feels put down by Wood.

Are You a Gold Personality?

Gold (pure type): positive. Oblong face, pale coloring. You are a superfortunate, one of life's chosen. But you need strength.

Pair with the stable Earth or the flexible Water.

Gold-Earth (mixed type): positive. Oblong face, tawny skin. This is a fortunate combination; you may not reach as high in status as pure Gold, because a part of you is rooted into the soil, but you will have security and honesty as well as charm. Pair with an Earth-Gold or a pure Earth type for security.

Gold-Water (mixed type): positive. Oblong face, swarthy skin. You gain flexibility, will become richer and have protection from Fire in this combination. Choose a Water mate for an interesting life, though you play a supportive role. You will be enriched by it. Avoid Fire-Earth.

Gold-Wood (mixed type): inharmonious. Oval face, fair or olive skin. This is a somewhat unfortunate combination, although you may not realize it until late in life. It gives beauty, but some weakness later on. Pair with Water, which helps Wood and to which you are supportive.

Gold-Fire (mixed type): inharmonious. Pear-shape face, ruddy skin. The Fire in you may negate your better qualities, and you may have to fantasize the kind of life Gold is chosen for rather than enjoy it in reality. Choose an Earth type, which helps Gold, and which is benefited by Fire. Avoid the pure Fire type, which can only burn you.

5. THE SAGACIOUS WOOD PEOPLE

Planet: Jupiter. Element: Wood. Color: green. Vitality: rising. Fortune: wisdom. Face shape: triangle. Complexion: olive. Helped by Water; helps Fire; hindered by Gold; detracts from Earth.

Wood is associated with the planet Jupiter, the largest in the solar system, just as it is in Western astrology. Its Vitality is rising—as a tree rises into the sky. Its Fortune is wisdom; it is the element of the sage, the seer, wisewoman and wiseman.

The Wood Face. The Wood face is a triangle, narrow at the bottom, widening to a broad forehead. Often the forehead is also high; the ears and the nose can be long; the eyes are elegant and the eyebrows are clear. The hair on the head is not too thick, and males with this face have a thin beard. Usually the Wood type is tall and thin—but there actually are two types:

The A type is tall, big and bony, and this is the stronger type, like the sturdy oak.

The B type is thin and small, and this type is weaker. It is like the birch tree, not developing much girth.

The Wood Personality. The Wood type is spiritual. He or she is the most honest of the elemental types. Wood people are idealistic, with strong integrity. Because the Vitality of Wood is rising, they push up like a tree from a slender trunk and spread their branches into the sky. They enjoy expansion and soon soar above the mundane, often ending up on a higher plane than others aspire to. The Wood people see farther and in a broader range than others and expand intellectually and spiritually, drawing the rest of the world with them. They aspire to learn the secrets of the universe and are often out of this world.

Wood Vitality. The Vitality of Wood is rising, so Wood people tend to have their heads in the clouds. They are high-minded, altruistic.

Wood Fortune. The Fortune of Wood people is wisdom, so artists, scientists and thinkers are of this element. They tend to be worldly in nonmaterialistic matters and may not earn much money—but they are rich in knowledge and understanding.

Wood Combinations

- If Wood has a swarthy complexion, it is carrying Water, and this helps Wood find a better financial situation.
- If Wood has a ruddy complexion, particularly if the face is diamond shaped, it is a Wood-Fire combination. As Wood helps Fire, you may enjoy the showmanship in your personality and be more extroverted than the Wood type usually is.
- If Wood has a tawny complexion, perhaps a lozenge-shape face and large head, Wood is carrying Earth. The individual tends to have literary talents but may not be very aggressive. Wood-Earth tries to control or manipulate but will not be totally strong, as Wood cannot fight the negative effect of Earth's practicality upon Wood's dreaminess.
- With an oval face and an ivory coloring, a Wood individual carries Gold, and this is not a harmonious combination. Gold hinders Wood's idealism and intellect and can turn the person into a dilettante.

Wood People Pairups

Wood types undoubtedly do pair with each other, but particularly in this match, there is a lack of ballast. Two Wood types could go off together to an ivory tower, but who would buy the groceries?

- Wood is best paired with Water, who is supportive in many senses, particularly financially.
- Wood also pairs well with Fire, because the outgoing, extroverted Fire is helped by the inward, intellectual Wood and indeed gathers fuel from the relationship to keep the flame burning.
- As a highbrow and a thinker, Wood detracts from the strong and stable qualities of Earth—the industrialist— whose mind is forever on developments. As we have seen, a conflict between Wood and Earth is very real in our present-day society.
- Wood is hindered by Gold—in the way the elite (Gold) often neglect those who are not in their inner circle and fail to appreciate the extent to which their comforts and pleasures depend on the inventions and intellectual efforts of Wood.

Are You a Wood Personality?

Wood (pure type): positive. Triangle face, olive complexion. A balanced personality. You are one of the superfortunates. You need to be offset, though, by another element and should choose Water or Fire.

Wood-Water (mixed type): harmonious. Heart-shape face; swarthy coloring. Though there are very positive aspects to this combination, and Water helps Wood, the strength may diminish in later life. Pair with a Water sign to reinforce these energies and get more support.

Wood-Fire (mixed type): positive. Diamond-shape face, ruddy complexion. This creates great intelligence, with talents that can be used. The person is competitive but not materialistic. Choose to pair with Wood or Fire.

Wood-Earth (mixed type): negative. Triangular face, tawny complexion. You tend to deny and reject the practical side of your nature, so you may never achieve the goals your Wood personality sets. A Fire partner will help support the Earth element in you, and you will be supportive of the Fire partner.

Wood-Gold (mixed type): negative. Oval face, olive complexion. The Gold negates your high-minded Wood nature, and the vitality of Gold—grace—and its high status do not provide the practicality you need. You may have beauty, but there will be weakness, too. As Gold helps Water, you may do best with a Water pairup.

GUIDELINES TO DETERMINING THE ELEMENTAL TYPES

Because understanding the elemental type to which you or another belongs is so important to evaluating the personality, and because so many of us are mixed types, you may need additional guidelines in distinguishing the basic element from other elements being carried.

Bear in mind that all *pure* types are relatively rare, and in our present stage of development, pure Fire types are the rarest. Pure Earth and pure Water types occur most frequently, while pure Gold and pure Wood types are somewhere in between. Of combination types, Wood-Fire, Wood-Gold and Wood-Water appear relatively often.

When you are in doubt, look at the following chart, which shows a complete breakdown of the physical characteristics of each elemental type. Count the characteristics of each type that are found in the individual. The person will usually show the greatest number of characteristics of his or her basic elemental type and will be carrying the element or elements indicated by the other characteristics.

PHYSICAL CHARACTERISTICS

	Fire	*Water*
Face shape	conic	round
Complexion	ruddy	swarthy
Skin	dry	moist
Hair	curly	thick
Ears	pointed	thick, solid
Eyes	sparkling	luminous
Features	pointed	rounded
Structure	bony	fleshy
Flesh	tight	loose
Physique	wiry	rounded
Posture	alert	relaxed
Gestures	quick	flowing
Voice	hoarse	resonant

An important point to remember about complexion color is that all the various elemental types appear with similar frequency in all nationalities and ethnic groups. It is probable that at the origin of the idea of elemental types (lost in antiquity), the five elements represented the five major ethnic groupings of human-kind. So, on the basis of related complexion color and other characteristics, it is easy to jump to the conclusion that each elemental type still represents a specific ethnic group. But this is not true. Each of the elemental types was recognized among the Chinese themselves. And just as Orientals and Caucasians can have ivory (Gold), swarthy (Water), ruddy (Fire), olive (Wood) and tawny (Earth) complexions, so Amerinds and blacks have similar variations. However, in an Amerind or a black individual, the Gold type (ivory) complexion, for example, will not neces- sarily be so much lighter in color as finer in texture, with a luminescence and translucent quality, as of polished onyx or copper, that is readily apparent to observers. So also the ruddy, swarthy, tawny and olive (grayish-green) variations can be seen in these ethnic groups.

OF ELEMENTAL TYPES

Earth	*Wood*	*Gold*
square	triangular	oblong
tawny	olive	ivory
solid	tight	dewy
coarse	straight	fine
large	triangular, thin	round, small
sharp	clear	bright
large	long	delicate
muscled	knobby	well-modeled
heavy	firm	smooth
stocky	lean	well-proportioned
massive	erect/willowy*	composed
slow	sweeping	graceful
deep	clear	melodious

*Note: There are two wood types. See pages 36–37.

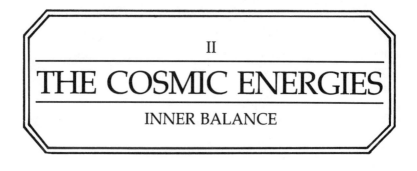

II

THE COSMIC ENERGIES

INNER BALANCE

The universe, according to Chinese teaching, is comprised of two cosmic energies—positive, creative *Yang* (Sun) and receptive *Yin* (Moon).

Yang represents the positive, masculine, creative force of light (Sun) in the universe and so relates to the aggressive part of the personality, the energy involved in creating a place for ourselves in the world—in the development of character, in the exercise of power and control in areas in which we are dominant and active. For most of us, this represents our work. (Aggressiveness in this sense should not be equated with violence and hostility, which result, instead, from the frustration of aggressive drives.)

The Yin force relates to the emotional and pleasurable aspects of the individual. The ability to relax and enjoy life comes from Yin. Yin is related to how we spend our leisure time, our home life, our pleasures and our relationships with spouse and children. (The home is Yin as the workplace is Yang; the interior decorations and soft parts of the house are Yin.)

Note that although the aggressive drive (Yang) is associated with the masculine qualities of the personality, it is not exclusive to the male sex. Both men and women have Yang and Yin in their natures. The traditional life-style of the male may, however, emphasize the Yang and that of the woman the Yin. It is the balance of these two cosmic energies that creates a harmonious individual.

In the face, the bony structure is Yang; the soft parts, including the flesh and skin, are Yin.

As a general rule, all *prominent* bones in the face and head are Yang and are considered fortunate, but of particular good fortune are a bony forehead (called Wisdom Yang) and pro-tuberances on each side of the forehead. The places where the cheekbones connect with the skull on each side of the head, beside the temples, are called the Sun Bones. Prominences here also are fortunate.

When you are observing the face, look at the bony structure and for the prominence of the bony (Yang) features—the fore-head, cheekbones, nose, chin and jawbones. Also check the firmness of the flesh, the smoothness of the skin and the fleshy areas of the face—the tip of the nose, the mouth—which are Yin. If the flesh is saggy or puffy or if the skin is loose and lined, this indicates diminished Yin energy. On the other hand, exposed bones with little flesh and taut skin also show diminished Yin qualities. The bone structure (Yang) should be prominent but softened by firm flesh and smooth skin (Yin), indicating har-mony between the cosmic energies.

The face as a whole is considered to be Yang (Sun), while the part covered by hair is Yin (Moon). When divided into two sides, the left side is Yang; the right side is Yin. The left side thus represents the father and masculine, paternal (Yang) influences in the individual, and the right side represents the mother and maternal, feminine (Yin) influences in the personality.

In observing a face, the sides of the face should be balanced to assure the balance of cosmic energy. If one side or another is dominant, if the face is somehow unbalanced or crooked, it indicates an imbalance in the influence of the significant parent and often an overemphasis of the positive, aggressive, mas-culine, paternal, Yang qualities (left side) or of the receptive, emotional, maternal, feminine, Yin qualities (right side), depend-ing on which side is dominant. Of course, no face has two sides completely identical, but some faces have differences that are readily apparent, for example, a tendency to lift one eyebrow or to smile to one side of the face, one eye larger than the other, a dimple on one side but not on the other, a scar or mole, etc.

When you are observing the face, look for a balance between the Yang and Yin qualities—bony structure and flesh, balance in the sides of the face, balance in the amount of the head that is exposed (face, Yang) and that is covered with hair (Yin). This balance shows harmony in the individual—one who is capable of balancing the aggressive and pleasure drives in his or her nature.

If the individual is Yang dominant (prominent features, exposed bones, little flesh), the person will often show a need to control others, may drive too hard for power and success and may be afflicted with work addiction. If Yin is dominant (small features, hidden bones, fleshy), the person may be submissive, underachieving, overemotional and given to self-indulgence.

The balanced personality harmonizes the aggressive (Yang) and pleasure (Yin) drives, and this allows one to work successfully and also to enjoy one's home and leisure.

GUIDELINES

- Observe the balance between the open parts of the head (face, Yang) and the part of the head covered with hair (Yin). The hair should not grow too far down at the sides or forehead nor very far down at the back of the head. Balding in the young (under 40) indicates disharmony in Yin and Yang.
- Observe the bony (Yang) structure of the face. Are the features that should be prominent—forehead, nose, cheekbones, jaw, chin—in fact prominent? Or are they small, hidden by flesh or flat, the face too smooth?
- Observe the Yin (soft) parts of the face. Is the flesh firm? Is the skin smooth and firm? Or are the bones all exposed, with tight skin, little flesh?
- Observe the balance of the left (Yang) and the right (Yin) sides of the face. Are they in harmony or is one side dominant?
- As a general rule, *all prominent bones* on the face are considered fortunate.

III

THE THREE STATIONS

INNER HARMONY

Basically, the face represents the layout of the Imperial Court. The Chinese imperial compound was divided into three major areas, or stations. At the highest level—the upper elevation—were the family living quarters, schools and temples of the ancestors. The middle elevation held the government buildings, the throne rooms and the temples of the sun and moon. The lower level—the third elevation—was the place of commerce, reception areas, servants' quarters and storage places. Each area represented a major function of court, and the three were balanced for harmony in everyday living.

The face, similarly, is divided lengthwise into three stations, each representing a major part of life:

- The First Station, the top part of the face from the hairline to the middle of the eyebrows, represents youth (age 14 through 30).
- The Second Station, the midsection of the face from the middle of the eyebrows to the bottom of the nose, represents mid-life (age 31–50).
- The Third Station, the lower part of the face, from the bottom of the nose to the tip of the chin, represents

maturity (age 50 and after).
• Childhood (conception to age 13) is represented by the ears.

If the stations are balanced—all three stations of equal length—it indicates a balanced life—and that each of the three major life phases will be productive and contribute to a well-rounded life scenario. Background and education (First Station) will lead to achievement in middle life (Second Station), resulting in a comfortable and satisfying maturity (Third Station).

If one station is dominant, it indicates the part of life in which the individual will be most effective and to which he or she will be most closely oriented. The weakest (shortest) station indicates the part of life in which you will have most of your problems. But remember that the fortunes of each station bear upon the fortunes of the next one you enter. A dominant First Station doesn't mean that life is over at thirty. In fact, the proper use of the fortunate early years can provide the resources to carry you over any rough spots in the Second Station. And a dominant Second Station can do much to secure comfort for the less productive later years of the Third Station.

Let's explore in more detail the significance of each station and its bearing on your life as a whole and also indicate what to look for when you observe the stations of another person's face.

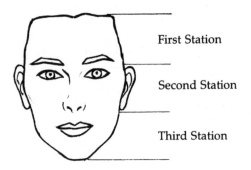

First Station

Second Station

Third Station

1. FIRST STATION—YOUTH

The First Station embraces the top of the face from hairline to middle of the eyebrows and represents the years from age fourteen through thirty. It holds only one feature—the forehead. The First Station represents preparation for life and has to do with background, parental influence, education, mentality and attitudes toward life. The years represented by this station are those when the influences of family background and the effort to get an education and develop one's mind, to choose a vocation and form relationships, are most important. Relationships developed in these years are often the most influential in deciding what the future will be like.

Ideally, the First Station should be fairly high and broad, clear (unlined) and, for success, with bony protuberances. It is better domed (slightly rounded), not flat. This indicates fine intellect, good family background, the chance to get a good education and to form beneficial relationships. But keep in mind that balance— the relationship among the three stations—is what creates harmony. Many people have a dominant First Station and many others have a short First Station. If so, they lack this balance.

- If the First Station is dominant (more prominent than the others), the person often has success in the first third of life (before age 30). For example, the eldest child in a family usually has a high forehead and often gets the best education and the most help from the parents. If a child has a dominant First Station and is not the eldest, the child may have to take responsibility for the parents at an early age.
- If the First Station is short, flat and narrow, the person often gets off to a poor start, has little help from the parents and perhaps has trouble getting an education or even training for a job. However, this person, if the Second Station is strong, may achieve great success in the middle years, and the benefits of this may last, if the Third Station is strong, into the later years. Again, however, it is the balance among the stations that is to be looked for if the life is to be harmonious.

Note that men over forty or even younger often have a receding hairline that may make the forehead seem higher and the First Station longer in relation to other stations than it actually is. This kind of balding after age forty indicates intellectual growth. Similarly, hairpieces sometimes lower the natural hairline and make the forehead seem lower than it is. Be observant.

2. SECOND STATION—MID-LIFE

The Second Station runs from the middle of the eyebrows to the bottom of the nose. It represents mid-life—the years from thirty-one to fifty—and has to do with the individual's capabilities, wealth and achievement—the business of living. Four major features (eyebrows, eyes, nose, even ears) are in this station, along with two minor features (the undereye area and the cheekbones).

- A dominant Second Station—with prominent mountains (forehead, nose, cheekbones)—indicates a success oriented and often self-made individual, frequently one who is achievement addicted and who may sacrifice himself or herself to a career or to assuring the security of home and family.
- If a dominant Second Station is flat, it indicates one who will work hard but be less achievement oriented or whose achievement falls short of his or her goals.
- A short Second Station indicates one who must look for success in the earlier or later period of life—or perhaps one who will not be interested in worldly success or public achievement. Many worthy individuals are not.
- A weak Second Station, both short and flat, shows one who will be at the mercy of fluctuations in the economy and social change during the period of the adult years and may not realize youthful dreams or not be able to guarantee security for later life.
- A balanced, well-formed Second Station is an indicator of achievement and a promise of success in the middle years, as well as of one who will integrate work and family life. It shows one who is a good provider both by securing the means for a good life for the family and also by nurturing the household.

Note that prominent mountains, particularly a prominent nose, may make the Second Station appear more dominant than it actually is. Or the nose, if it is long, sometimes casts a shadow that may make the Second Station seem longer than it actually is, while a short or upturned nose with exposed nostrils may make the Second Station appear shorter than it is. Take care to evaluate the length of the stations correctly.

3. THIRD STATION—MATURITY

The Third Station runs from the bottom of the nose to the tip of the chin and represents the last third of life—the years after fifty. It shows the fruits of living. One major feature—the mouth—and four important minor features—chin, jawbones, laughlines and philtrum (the groove from the bottom of the nose to the upper lip)—fall into this station.

The third part of life, represented by the Third Station, is the period during which achievement and aggressive drive become less significant, and the security and status you have achieved are now increasingly important.

Ideally, the Third Station should be balanced with the other stations for a satisfactory and comfortable old age. In observing a youthful face, bear in mind that the Third Station is the slowest to mature and may not reach its full strength till age thirty or later.

- If the Third Station is dominant—longer than each of the other two stations—the individual may be a late bloomer and find success and happiness only in the later years. If the chin area, however, is long and pointed, it shows a tendency to dominate others in old age, and this can lead to loneliness.
- If the Third Station is weak—shorter than the other stations and flat—it shows weakness, perhaps immaturity in maturity, perhaps poverty or illness in old age or a lack of the status necessary to make life rewarding.
- A balanced Third Station shows the carrying over of the harmony of life into the last period of life—maturity. And if other features bear this out, it usually indicates a comfortable old age and long life.

4. EVALUATING THE STATIONS

An evaluation of the Three Stations can tell you at a glance a great deal about yourself or another, primarily the quality of life in the three major periods—youth, mid-life and maturity. It can also indicate whether an individual will have his or her best years in youth, middle or old age. But again, do not be too judgmental right off.

The nature of the Three Stations shows problems to be overcome along with strengths and weak points, and each station is modified by the quality and type of the features and other significators it contains: the quality of the early years by boniness, roundness or flatness as well as the shape of the forehead and hairline; success in the middle years by the shape of the nose, cheekbones and so on; the quality of later years by the firmness of the chin and jawline.

And of course the station you now inhabit because of your present age is of greater significance in the present scheme of things. The shape of the face actually changes as you go through life. The Third Station, for example, may not be mature until after age thirty. On the other hand, the Third Station may actually weaken in later life—through loss of teeth or bone. The First Station may lengthen in males through a receding hairline. The Second Station may strengthen as we exercise power.

However, by observing the three stations, you can evaluate the period of life in which most energy will be expended, the prospects of the person in youth, middle and old age and the harmony (balance) of the personality.

GUIDELINES

- The stations are primarily lengthwise divisions of the face.
- The First Station—from hairline to mid-brow—represents youth (ages 14–30) and concerns intellect, background and parental influence. It represents Mars (Fire Star) and is involved with the adventure of life.
- The Second Station—from mid-brow to bottom of nose— represents mid-life (ages 31–50) and concerns achievement. It represents the Saturn (Earth Star) influence, the stabilization of life through work, family and the use of one's capacities.
- The Third Station—from bottom of nose to tip of chin— represents life from age fifty on, and concerns health, maturity, results of achievement, children and grandchildren. It represents the influence of Mercury (Water Star) and has to do primarily with adjustments.
- If all stations are balanced (of equal length), it indicates harmony in the individual and in the life context.

- If any one station is dominant, it indicates the period during which the energies will be most powerful.
- If any one station is weak, it indicates the period during which the individual will have problems or be deprived.
- Your present age indicates which station is most significant to you now. However, you can look ahead to the quality of life as you enter the other stations or look back on how the past is influencing your present.

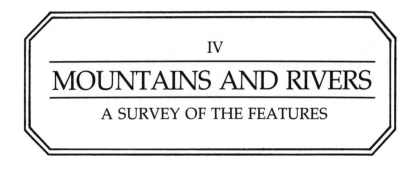

IV

MOUNTAINS AND RIVERS

A SURVEY OF THE FEATURES

The ancient Chinese saw the face as a reflection of the layout of the Imperial Court, so the face, like the grounds or terrain of the empire, is seen as being composed of mountains and rivers. The mountains are the forehead, nose, cheekbones and chin. These are the naturally outstanding features and, ideally, as mountains, should be prominent. The mountains are, of course, the bony features associated with the active cosmic energy Yang, and so it is valuable for success in the aggressive sphere of life to have *all* these features prominent. A *single* outstanding prominent feature is not considered balanced. A mountain needs to be supported by other mountains.

The forehead is a mountain. A forehead bulge is called Going for Gold, indicating a strong urge toward the finer things of life. A column of bone running down the middle of the forehead is, as we shall see, an indicator of success. Sometimes there is a prominent bony structure or bulge on both sides of the forehead. This shows ability to achieve a high position in life. Sometimes the bones underlying the eyebrows are prominent. Although these are not considered natural mountains, they indicate an important claim to fame.

The nose is often the most prominent mountain. Forehead, cheekbones and chin should also be prominent, not flat, leaving the nose alone on a plain. A flat nose in any type is an indicator of a need to work hard, no matter how strong the surrounding mountains.

A knobby chin, a mountain, is of value, for the chin represents strength and thus is a great aid in longevity. A flat chin weakens the chance for sustaining health and vitality in old age; a long, pointed chin indicates one who seeks to dominate others and consequently becomes lonely in old age.

As with everything in the Chinese philosophy, a balanced terrain, with all the mountains prominent but none dominating the others, is ideal, because it enables one to balance the characteristics they represent—character (forehead), power (cheekbones), wealth (nose) and strength (chin).

The rivers are the moisture-producing features—ears, eyes, nostrils, mouth. These are all soft, fleshy features and are of the nature of the cosmic energy Yin—emotional, receptive, feminine. Because they are rivers, these features should appear moist.

GUIDELINES

You will, of course, later be observing the Five Major Features and Seven Minor Features in detail (see parts Three and Four). At first glance, an indication of the prominence of the mountains and the dryness or moisture of the rivers gives a preliminary insight into character and personality.

V

PLANET POINTS

VIGOR AND GOOD FORTUNE

Certain features hold *planet points*, meaning the relevant feature *represents* a particular planet and takes on its coloring. Appropriate coloring indicates good health, vitality and balanced energies.

Each planet is related not only to a certain color but also to a special Fortune and Vitality. Checking the coloring at the planet points also offers a guide to the fortunes of a specific enterprise and to the generating of the kind of Vitality needed for success. If the feature's color is appropriate, the Vitality is strong and your fortunes will prosper. If the color is wrong at any particular time, Vitality will be impeded and fortunes will be adversely affected.

The planet points, their location, appropriate colors, Fortune and Vitality are:

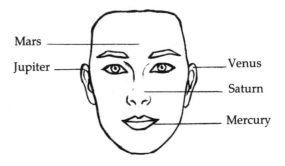

Jupiter (Wood Star)—right ear; wisdom.

Venus (Gold Star)—left ear; status. The appropriate color for the ears is pinky white, lighter than the face. If the ears are too red or too ashen, this is unlucky. Consult the ears for matters requiring good judgment (right ear) and a rise in standing or chance of loss of status (left ear).

Mars (Fire Star)—forehead; pink; adventure; activity. The forehead should be pinkish, no matter what the complexion color. If the forehead is too red, it indicates rashness; if it is too light, it shows diminution of energy for activities. The Fortune of Mars is adventure and its Vitality is activity, so consult your forehead for matters that involve daring and showmanship, and that require physical action.

Saturn (Earth Star)—nose; golden tan; security; stillness. No matter what the complexion color, the nose should be golden tan. If the nose is too reddish, it is not wholesome for stabilization and achievement; if it is greenish or grayish, it shows diminished health. Because the Fortune of Saturn is security and its Vitality is stillness, consult the nose for matters involving emotional and economic security and also matters that require patience and waiting.

Mercury (Water Star)—mouth; red; wealth; flexibility. The color of Mercury is black, and so the mouth should be deep red, not too pale or too purplish. The Fortune of Mercury is wealth and its Vitality is flexibility. So consult the mouth for money deals and for matters that require rapid adjustment and a flexible attitude.

Because the coloring of these planet points is also a health indicator (Vitality), they can be used as a quick checkup to be sure your physical vitality is up to par.

GUIDELINES

Observe the planet points not only in yourself but also in others with whom you are involved: in your partners, employers, employees, mate, children and parents. The coloring of the planet points can tell you whether another is operating at optimum vitality and if his or her fortune is likely to be benign in any enterprise you engage in together.

THE STAR POINTS

VI

INNER GLOW

Inner glow shows the *heart* of the individual—the quality that makes a person appear attractive no matter what the features are like. The inner glow is especially apparent in the *star-point* area of the face, though it often pervades the entire face and gives a beautiful luminosity to the whole personality.

The star points—there are six—are also areas to check for the prospect of success of various kinds: in youth for the promise or future they hold for you; later, for the rewards you can expect. The star points can be checked daily for assurance about prospects in everyday life.

The star points are particularly glowing in those who have innate "star quality"—the ability to become a star performer in any chosen field. This is not limited to showmanship, politics, sports or the arts. You can become a star in finance, business, medicine, education or whatever. You can be a star pupil, a star parent, a star worker, a star friend or a star companion.

The star points are areas rather than specific points. Each eyebrow is a star point. The left eyebrow is the Baron or Overlord; the right eyebrow is the Counselor. Each eye is a star point. The left eye is Sun Star; the right eye is Moon Star. The other star points are the area between the brows (Purple Air) and the area between the eyes (Moon Dust).

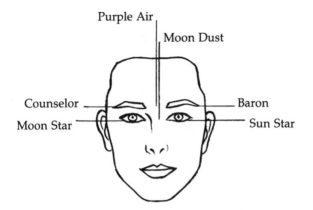

Purple Air
Moon Dust
Counselor
Baron
Moon Star
Sun Star

1. THE BARON AND THE COUNSELOR

As star points, the eyebrows indicate the aggressive inner drive an individual needs to become a star—to achieve fame in any field. The Baron, or Overlord, the left eyebrow, indicates stardom through your own enterprise and aggressiveness; the Counselor, the right eyebrow, supports this drive with wise direction of enterprise and acuity in making your own luck.

In face reading, the eyebrows are considered violent stars and should be kept out of other star territory. It is unfortunate if the brows grow together (joined above the nose), because this puts violent stars in contact, and they might thus self-destruct. If they grow too close together, they also invade the important territory of star point Purple Air between the brows. Men as well as women should remove hairs from the between-the-brows area, both because they will then *appear* less violent and because Purple Air will be free to function for success.

As star points, the eyebrows are auguries of success when the hairs are silky and strong, smooth and of good color, and when the eyebrows are arched, reasonably long and neither too thick nor too thin and of a distinctive shape. The world's stars have eyebrows that are clearly defined, strong and distinctive.

Of course, most women and many men today shape their eyebrows, so they often are not easy to evaluate. If you are shaping your own, bear in mind that what detracts from their promise is straggly hairs, brows growing too close together or joined over the nose, uneven color, loose hairs that stand up from the line of the brow, weak color or sparse eyebrow hair. The ideal width between the brows is the width of two fingers, unless the eyes are very close set. Then the width of one and a half fingers is ideal.

It is vital for those who hope to star in the entertainment world or politics or in other spheres of public life to have strong, distinctive eyebrows, for the brows as a feature indicate fame.

2. PURPLE AIR

The star point Purple Air lies in the area between the brows. This area holds the Seal of Approval. It shows the blessing of heaven upon success and is the signal of that intangible known as star quality. It is, in particular, the significator of those who are born to success—often early, *easy* success, as if they were destined to be winners.

This area should be fairly wide (two fingers' width between the brows, as we have seen) and free of hair. In those who are blessed with this Seal of Heaven, the area will have a kind of purplish glow. Sometimes this seal appears as a round, purplish spot in young children, indicating that they are indeed the darling of the gods. However, at any time in life, if this area takes on a purplish coloring, you are likely to have success in any enterprise that is under way.

3. SUN STAR AND MOON STAR

The eyes are each a star point—the left eye is Sun Star and the right eye is Moon Star. As star points, the eyes grant stardom through creativity, intelligence and inner vitality, and through the balance and effective use of the cosmic energies Yang (Sun) and Yin (Moon).

For star quality, the eyes should be fairly large, luminous and moist, with a large iris and the white of the eye very clear. The white should not show above or below the iris (the colored part of the eye). The flesh around the eye should be firm and the skin unlined. Flatness and any discoloration are not fortunate.

Most significant for star quality is light, or sparkle, in the eyes. If they appear dull, reddish or yellowish, or if the glitter is too hectically bright, it is not a good time to seek success in the areas indicated by these star points—creativity, enterprise, ventures requring ingenuity and acute intelligence and intuition.

4. MOON DUST

The star point Moon Dust lies between the eyes just above the root of the nose. Just as the star point Purple Air grants easy success in youth as the gift of heaven, Moon Dust promises success in later years through concentrated effort and ambition. This star point represents the aptitudes and talents necessary to achieve stardom and the diligence to work to achieve one's dream. Stardom achieved through this star point Moon Dust usually lasts well into maturity, even through all of life.

To promise stardom, the space occupied by Moon Dust should be fairly wide, with the width of one eye between the eyes. This area ideally is smooth and rounded, not deeply indented, and clear of lines. The favorable color is clear and light, not greenish or yellowish or dark.

Radiance in the star-point areas is characteristic of those who star in life. This kind of clarity and glow are noticeable in children of great promise, and they carry over in those who star at any age. But even for those who do not become stars in their field—be it business, finance, theater, politics, the military, the arts or whatever—the star points should be checked whenever success is sought, for example, winning a competition, running for office, getting a promotion, marrying, becoming a parent or grandparent, getting an award, making the team, even passing an examination or giving a party. At some point in life, everyone has a chance to star. Checking the star points for possibilities of success can add to your confidence or protect you from disappointment.

GUIDELINES

- The Baron and the Counselor (the eyebrows) indicate the inner drive (daring) that brings stardom and fame. Keys are smoothness, strength, distinctive shape.
- Purple Air augurs success in youthful enterprises and indicates the blessing of heaven (luck) on any endeavor. The key is purplish coloring.

- Sun Star and Moon Star (the eyes) have to do with the inner energy (talent) that promotes success. Brilliance, smooth skin and clarity are the desired indicators.
- Moon Dust shows the ambition, integration and hard work necessary to develop talents. The keys are smoothness, clarity and good color.

VII

THE PALACES

CHECKPOINTS FOR ACTIVITIES

The face, like the compound, or grounds, of the Chinese Imperial Court, is occupied by *palaces*—areas in which the functions of the court, from the most celestial to the most mundane, are carried out. In the face, the palaces are areas to be checked for the probable outcome (good or ill fortune) of any significant life enterprise—marriage, love affairs, travel, money matters, real estate and so on. Regardless of what activity you plan, the enterprise will fall into the provenance of one of these palaces. You can check the state of any particular palace at any time to preview your possibilities for a successful action.

If the color is glowing and appropriate to the area occupied by the particular palace in which you are interested, your promise of success is strong. If the area appears dull, the color is wrong for the area, or the palace appears sunken, dark or blemished, you are warned of possible disappointment and perhaps should delay your venture or take an alternative course.

Basically there are twelve palaces. Those appearing in the middle of the face are single. However, those that lie on the sides of the face are double, each of the two palaces having a slightly different significance. So there are twenty of these checkpoints in all. Bear in mind when there are two palaces—a summer palace

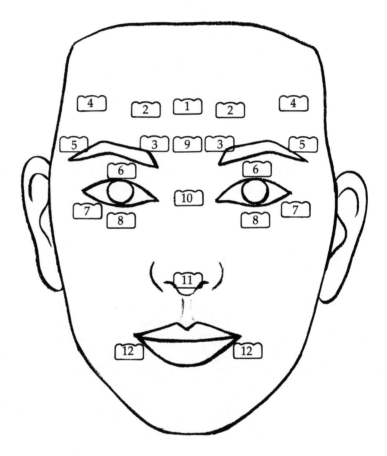

and a winter palace, so to speak—relating to the enterprise engaging your attention, that the one on the left side will be of the nature of Yang (positive, outgoing, active), while the one on the right will be of the nature of Yin (receptive, passive). This will be elucidated as we discuss the various palaces.

1. PALACE OF ACHIEVEMENT

The Palace of Achievement runs down the middle of the forehead from the hairline to just above the top line of the eyebrows. This area is also called the Pathway of Heaven. Sometimes a column of bone runs down this palace, and this bone is called the Column of Heaven, an indicator of high achievement. Because this palace is on the forehead, a feature that represents Mars (Fire Star), whose color is red, the favorable color here is a pinkish glow. If you have a Column of Heaven, it may seem to stand out more or deepen in color when success in an enterprise is augured. On the other hand, if this area becomes pale or is dark or mottled, it warns against making a bid for success at this particular time. Wait for a more auspicious moment.

2. PALACES OF PARENTS

There is a palace for each parent, the Palace of the Father on the left and the Palace of the Mother on the right. These palaces lie to the left and right of the Palace of Achievement on each side of the upper forehead. Sometimes you'll find bony protuberances here, indicating a rich endowment or heritage from the parents. For matters concerning your father or your father's side of the family, consult the palace on the left side. For matters concerning your mother or your mother's side of the family, consult the palace on the right. If a family conference is in order, consult both sides.

Although these palaces are indicators of matters relating directly to the parents, they also are indicators of matters concerning your background, education and preparation for career. For example, you would consult these areas about the prospects of passing an exam, filing an application for college entrance or getting a letter of recommendation. Again, as these palaces are on the forehead, which represents Mars, a pink glow is promising; if the area is pale or too red, you are warned of problems and should take precautions.

3. PALACES OF FRIENDS AND SIBLINGS

Again there are two—the Palace of Friends on the left and of Siblings on the right. Friends are Yang, for these are relationships you choose; while siblings are Yin, because you receive your brothers and sisters in the natural course of events. These palaces lie on the lower forehead, just above the inner tips of the eyebrows on each side. A kind of bony protuberance there indicates social success. Consult the Palace of Friends, left, for matters concerning friendship and also social activities, dependence on influential connections, in a sense "friends at the court," as well as for purely social activities. The Palace of Siblings (right) involves not only natural brothers and sisters but fraternal and sororal organizations. Again, for a happy outcome of an enterprise, the wholesome color here is a pinkish glow. Pallor or a darkening in the area suggests you defer social engagements or use exquisite tact in dealing with friends or siblings at the time.

4. PALACES OF TRANSFER

There are two, called the Stagecoaches because they are concerned with the auspices of travel and movement from place to place, as well as with the transfer of goods and property. These palaces lie on the outer forehead, above the outer tip of the eyebrows, and fan outward and upward to the hairline at the temple. The palace on the left indicates your own travels and ventures, goods shipped out, even outgoing mail, anything that is moved out from you to another point, and in a sense also goods that are lost or stolen. It also concerns your vehicles—car, bike, and the like—in the sense that you use them for transportation. (Other aspects of your vehicle may fall under the Palaces of Property or the Household.) The Palace of Transfer on the right should be consulted for things that are moved to you—incoming visitors who travel to see you, mail or goods you receive or your *return* from a journey. So both Palaces of transfer should usually be consulted if you are planning a trip. Again, the appropriate color is a pinkish glow; dark or greenish coloring here indicates that plans will not go well and perhaps should be deferred or arrangements made with extreme precautions.

The Palaces of Transfer also concern explorations and adventures of the mind and the probing of your psyche to find your direction in life, and also relocation at a distance from your present home.

5. PALACES OF HAPPINESS AND GOOD FORTUNE

These palaces might be called the Casinos, for they are the areas a gambler should check before venturing. Again there are two, the Palace of Happiness (the luck you bring to yourself) on the left and the Palace of Good Fortune (the luck that falls in your lap) on the right. However, because we make our own luck in most cases, check both before you engage in games of chance or other affairs that are dependent on luck or whenever you hope to invite happiness and good fortune into your affairs. At times, it is so important to be in the right place at the right time, to meet "by chance" someone who changes your life for the better, or to do, without thinking, some minor thing that brings good fortune, that a check on these palaces is well worth your daily attention.

The Palaces of Happiness and Good Fortune lie at the outer tip of the eyebrows and extend to the hairline at the lower temple. A kind of glow or luminescence here and pinkish coloring indicate that your luck is favorable; dark coloring or greenish coloring warns against gambling till the area clears.

Are you naturally lucky? For some people, these palaces tell whether they are born lucky or unlucky. The temple area is, of course, a naturally hollow area in the head bone. If the upper temple, the area of the Palaces of Happiness and Good Fortune, is very deep and hollow and of darkish or greenish color, you could be one of those who says, "I've never won anything in my whole life." If, on the other hand, the area is rounded and well formed, with no sign of indentation and a glow of the color normal to your complexion, you could be naturally lucky. Too much of a flush or redness here is not salutary—it indicates a tendency to reckless gambling, warns of gambling addiction.

6. PALACES OF PROPERTY

There are two Palaces of Property, located in the fleshy part of the eye just below the eyebrows. People in the real-estate business often have a very full, fleshy formation in these underbrow areas. Check these palaces when you are considering buying or selling a house or other real property or making any major purchase—a car, for example, or furnishings, or making capital improvements on property (repairs and minor purchases come under the Palace of the Household, which follows). In buildings, it is important to remember that the structure of the house is Yang (palace on the left) and the interior decoration and furnishings are Yin (palace on the right).

The favorable condition for enterprises that concern the Palaces of Property is firmness and fullness of this fleshy part of the upper lid, with luminescence or glow, no lines and no discoloration. If the area is puffy, it does not augur well, for this indicates water accumulation, and possibly a purchase will cost you too much or the money aspect will somehow not work out well. Avoid buying and selling or other dealing in property when the area is droopy, overly dry and lined or discolored. If this area is naturally hollow and bony—it needs a covering of flesh for the accumulation of property—you might seek an agent or lawyer or other surrogate to handle your property, as you could be your own worst enemy.

Property coming to you through your father or your father's family is indicated by the Palace of Property under the left eyebrow; property coming to you through your mother or your mother's family is indicated by the Palace of Property under the right eyebrow.

7. PALACES OF MARRIAGE

Again, there are two, and they lie at the very outer corner of the eye in the crow's-foot area—so called because of the three tiny lines resembling the foot of a crow that often develop there. The outer tip of the left eye is the Palace of Wives and Children (marriage), and the outer tip of the right eye is the Palace of Concubines (extramarital affairs). Smooth Palaces of Marriages (unlined) give contentment, stability and fertility in marriage.

The more lines or crinkles you find here, the more marriages or extramarital affairs you can expect to indulge in.

This is, of course, a very important area to observe when you want to determine whether someone will be serious about marriage or will just be indulging in one more affair. It also reveals whether a possible mate will actually settle down or will continue to play the field. Of course, some eye lines are common as one grows older—and has more experience. However, in the young, a number of eye-corner crinkles indicates sexual promiscuity. Because cosmetic surgery to eliminate eye wrinkles is common for both men and women, you sometimes have to rely on other methods to determine the fidelity you can expect from a prospective mate.

8. PALACES OF OFFSPRING

The areas under each eye are the locale of the Palaces of Children. In old China, where more than one wife and any number of concubines were acceptable for the male, the area under the left eye indicated the children of the wife and the area under the right eye the children of concubines. In Western society, the distinction for either a man or a woman would more likely be that the children born to a marriage were indicated by the area under the left eye and that children acquired by remarriage—stepchildren—or by adoption would be indicated by the right eye. However, the distinction is relatively unimportant. The Palaces of Offspring indicate fertility, the prospect of having children and how you as a parent will treat them.

This area is known as the sleeping silkworm because, when it is slightly puffy with a slight pad of fat underlying the skin, it looks like a silkworm in its cocoon. This area is also considered one of the Seven Minor Features and will be discussed further in that category. As a checkpoint—as a palace—it indicates reproductive capacity, a basic sexual attractant. For example, this area is said to take on a special glow when a woman is pregnant. If it is hollow or dark in color, it indicates sexual overindulgence.

Its favorable state is to be slightly full but not overly puffy, of good, light color and unlined. If it's too puffy, it is negative for sexuality and sexual health. If it's too flat, it indicates low fertility, especially if greenish, grayish or purplish in color.

9. PALACE OF LIFE

This is the Palace of Vitality, occupying the space between the brows. As this is the most important area on the forehead—it is called the Seal of Approval and marks the coming of maturity—it is the area to be checked when you seek a rise in position or when you wish to initiate an important life change. It is, in a sense, the Palace of Destiny—where Fate can bless you and you can embark on a path of fame and good fortune. This palace indicates the inner energy and vitality you need to bring endeavors to a successful start (implying a successful conclusion). A purplish glow in this area is the key to success. Be wary if the area is too pale or if it is dark or greenish or otherwise discolored.

10. PALACE OF HEALTH

The Palace of Health is located between the eyes and is an indicator of physical well-being. Good color and smoothness signify health and the free flow of energy; a line or dull color can indicate fatigue or diminishing strength.

It is particularly important to check this palace when you are planning a physical change—a new weight-loss diet, an exercise regimen or a new medical treatment or course of medication—but also when you are about to undertake any enterprise or endeavor that is going to depend on physical strength and emotional vitality.

The significance of one's health in enabling one to carry through many accomplishments is obvious. The Palace of Health should be checked (along with other health signifiers) to warn one about undue fatigue, any rundown condition or a need to revitalize yourself emotionally. When this area indicates a diminution of health, it may be a good time to take a vacation and emphasize for a while the Yin (emotional, leisure) side of your life and to undertake other efforts to balance your cosmic energies.

11. PALACE OF WEALTH

The whole tip of the nose, including the nostrils, is occupied by the Palace of Wealth. The helpful color here is the color of

Saturn (Earth)—peachy pink or beigy tan. Too much red here can indicate impulsiveness and extravagance in the handling of money; if it is greenish, you may suffer money loss or other financial woes.

A full, round tip on the nose is considered promising for the making of money; however, you may not accumulate it if the color indicates extravagance or, if the nose is too pale, whitish or greenish, you may be too cautious to become truly wealthy.

Check this Palace of Wealth in whatever kind of money-making scheme you are planning—for example, if you intend to ask for a raise in pay, make an important sale, borrow or lend money, invest or reinvest and, along with the Palaces of Happiness and Good Fortune, if you gamble. The nose is, of course, a major feature, and more about the nose and its relation to wealth will come out later. As the Palace of Wealth, this area is the indicator of your financial situation at the moment.

12. PALACES OF THE HOUSEHOLD

The Palaces of the Household occupy both sides of the lower face below the outer ends of the lower lip to the chin. Originally these were called the Palaces of Slaves and Servants, and even if we no longer have slaves and servants, some of the implications of these designations still apply. These palaces have to do with the everyday business of living—personal care, managing the household, home repairs, food, heat, people who do things for you and things you do for yourself and others. It concerns services and budgets, small equipment and tools. It also concerns the management of your body, its mineral reserves and physical functioning and how this affects your everyday life. Lines here, often developing late in life, sagging skin or too much flatness may indicate problems both in the function of the body and of the life-style. Basically, this is the Palace of Management, so if you undertake a diet or an exercise regimen, the program falls in this palace, although it is initiated under the Palace of Health.

When you require a change in your life-style or when you need to make any adjustments in the everyday scheme of things, check this palace for your go-ahead or a warning to delay. It should also be checked when you seek services from others, employ help, offer services to others or have dealings with your superiors.

Everything in the business of living, from the major life events to the least and most humdrum, is embraced by one or another of the twelve palaces. If you plan to embark on any project—involving travel, finance or property, for example—check the state of the relevant palace before you make your move.

It is also a good idea to check the palaces frequently to observe where you should be putting your energies.

GUIDELINES

- Give some thought to the particular palace you should be consulting for an enterprise.
- It is the color, firmness and glow that indicate whether your venture is taking place under good auspices.

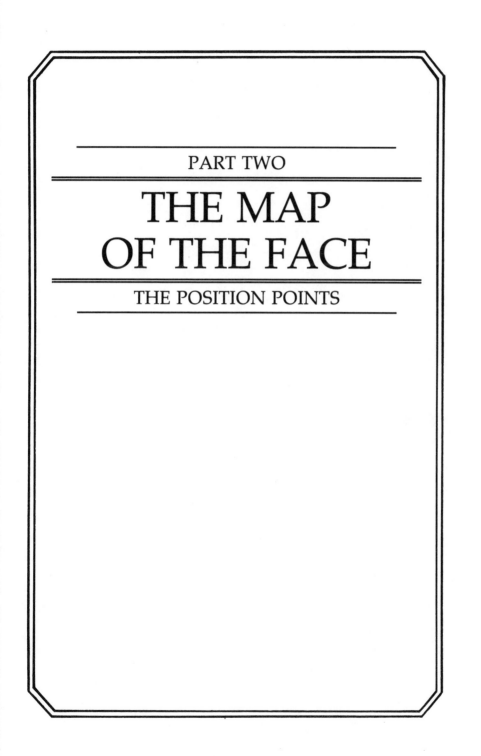

PART TWO

THE MAP
OF THE FACE

THE POSITION POINTS

THE HUNDRED POSITION POINTS

THE FLOATING YEAR

The *position points* of the *floating year* are among the most interesting aspects of the Chinese art of face reading, for they enable you to fix your position in life and learn the significance of the place at which you now stand through a study of your present age point. Each point represents a year in life and reveals some aspect of personality or destiny. From your present position point, you will discover the primary influences of your present year and the pursuits that are most favored at this particular time in your life. Consequently you will be better able to take advantage of the opportunities offered and also of your aptitudes, putting to work the energies that are currently most likely to be effective.

1. FINDING YOUR CURRENT POSITION POINT

Your current position point is your present age plus one. The Chinese measure life from conception, so you are at Position Point 1 on the day of your birth and Position Point 2 on your first birthday. Or, to think of it another way, on your first birthday, you start your second year of life and thus should be examining Position Point 2.

To find your present position point, add one to your age on your last birthday and then look for this point on the map of the face.

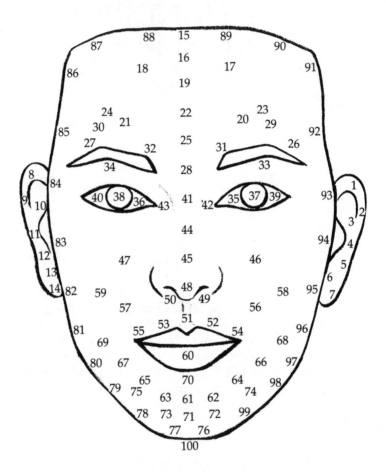

Points 1 to 14 are on the ears; Points 15 to 30 on the forehead. Points 31 to 34 are in the eyebrow and eye area (Points 35 to 40 are within the eye itself); Points 41 to 50 are on the nose; 46 and 47 are on the cheekbones; 51 to 55 are around the upper lip; Points 56 to 59 are on the cheeks. The mouth is Point 60. Points 61 to 75 are on the lower part of the face. The points from 76 to 100 run around the perimeter of the face and represent, as we shall see, not only a year in the life—that is, a floating year—but also the animal signs of the Chinese zodiac.

When you have found your position point, it is important to observe whether it is on the left side, on the right side or in the middle. You may find that when it is located on the left side, you are more subject to the influence of your father, more like your father's side of the family and more concerned with the Yang (aggressive) side of your life—for example, your work. When the position point falls on the right side, you are more like your mother and your mother's side of the family, more subject to maternal influence and also more concerned with the Yin (home, emotions and recreation) part of your life. When your position point falls in the middle, you are more likely to be your own person. Also observe in what station—the adventurous First Station (top of face), the stabilizing Second Station (middle face) or the flexible Third Station (lower part of the face)—it lies. Perhaps your present position point puts you in a star-point area, indicating a high point in your life, or it may fall on a major or minor feature, indicating which of your important characteristics will be emphasized at this period.

2. THE MEANING OF THE POSITION POINTS

The floating year is your current year of life. Each year you move to a new position point. As we have seen, the face represents a map of the Chinese Imperial Court. Just as the features represent mountains and rivers of the imperial terrain, the stations functional areas of the court, and the palaces areas of activities, the position points represent the places, or offices, of the various court officials. With each year, you move (float) from one office to another, and your responsibilities and experiences vary with your position.

The position point thus indicates opportunities you can take advantage of in your career and life-style. It spells out a personal attribute and destiny for each year and indicates whether you should be outgoing and aggressive about your goals or receptive, letting things come to you.

The position point is also an indication of your present vitality. If you are healthful and in good emotional balance, your position point should show a kind of luminescence or glow. It becomes another checkpoint for your well-being. Keep watching it. When it glows, you are probably in optimum health or emotional balance. If it seems dull greenish or pale or grayish, you may need physical care or emotional buoying up—and you can make life changes to bring yourself up to par. Although you may not at first be able to perceive anything special about this point, as you pay attention to it, it will become more responsive to your physical condition and emotional balance. If you have a scar, blemish or mole at your present position point, it may indicate a time to watch out for hazards or disappointments, depending on what the point signifies—for example, travel, sociability, health or career. If your present position point falls in a particular palace, the affairs indicated by that palace will be particularly significant to you.

You can also use your position point as a personal focus. You need not call attention to it in any particular way, but it is wise to think about it, even to meditate on its meaning, so that you will be unconsciously guided toward the promises it indicates. Consider it your focus for this particular year. In the following year, you will have another focus and enter into a new experience. Through the meaning of the position points, you can trace the future and plan ahead for more effective use of your time and energy. Looking back on your experiences at other position points, you may see the germination of changes and other important factors that affect your present life and so better understand your own particular destiny.

3. THE FORTUNES OF THE HUNDRED POSITION POINTS

As you will note, in addition to being associated with certain features, stations, palaces, star points and planet points, some of the position points are paired—like the Parent Points (17 and 18) and Rainbows (33 and 34). Such points suggest that you should evaluate the floating years represented by the two points in relation to each other—one will represent the outgoing, aggressive aspect of an enterprise, the other the receptive, emotional aspects.

The First Fourteen Points

The fourteen points of childhood lie on the ears—the ears, as a feature, represent life potential. The ears are each a planet point—the left ear represents Venus (Gold) and is called the Wheel of Heaven. The right ear represents Jupiter (Wood) and is called the Wheel of Humanity. Moving together, the two wheels create life.

Points 1 and 2 (conception to age 1)—Upper Wheel of Heaven. These points represent infancy from conception to the first birthday. As in all the left ear points,* the planet represented is Venus (Gold Star). The activity of Gold is grace; its fortune is status. Its sphere is management. These two points represent the rapid growth of the infant from a single cell to a bouncing 20-pound, 24-inch dynamo of energy.

Physical growth and mental and emotional development during this period are very quick, and in many ways, the temperament and personality of the child predict the kind of adult it will become. The ears, though they represent childhood, fall in the Second Station (mid-life), but in a general way (life potential), each ear represents the complete development of the individual. The Upper Wheel of Heaven is somehow comparable to the First Station of the face. The kind of start a child gets in life is observable from these two points.

Lines or marks at these points may indicate childhood traumas that will affect later life. The Personal Attribute is wonder; the Destiny is growth.

Points 3 and 4 (ages 2 and 3)—Middle Wheel of Heaven. These points represent the time the child learns to walk and talk and gain control over space and coordination of the physical body. It is again a period of rapid mental development. This is a stabilization period in early childhood, corresponding to the Second Station in adulthood.

---

*In the old tradition, the count for women begins on the Jupiter ear (right) and for men on the left ear (Venus). However, this tradition is often disregarded today.

At this time, a sense of identity—of belonging to the family emerges, bringing out the Yang characteristics associated with the father. The quality of life when the floating year is at these points probably tells much of the quality of life in the middle years. And the condition of these two points indicates the mental stability of the individual. The Personal Attribute of these two points is development and the Destiny is individualization.

Points 5, 6 and 7 (ages 4–6)—Pearl Drop of Heaven. The designation Pearl Drop indicates how precious the Chinese felt the earlobe to be. It represents longevity and wisdom, and is considered to hold important nerve centers related to the development of the brain. When the floating year is in these points, the child is determining the use of the life force and the development of thought. Usually the child is beginning school, separating from dependency on parents and acquiring independent judgment. This period relates to the integration of the Third Station. The condition of the Pearl Drop points indicates the prospect for long life and wisdom in old age. The Personal Attribute of the Pearl Drop of Heaven is knowledge and the Destiny is integration.

The right ear is called the Wheel of Humanity and represents the Planet Jupiter (Wood Star) with the attribute of rising as its Vitality and wisdom as its Fortune. It is the period when the Yin (maternal) qualities of arts, emotions and personality are most evident. It covers the period of later childhood, when the socialization of the child takes place.

Points 8 and 9 (ages 7, 8)—Upper Wheel of Humanity. This is the period in which the child accepts the direction of parents and the discipline of study and school and begins to reveal aptitudes, form friendships and explore the culture into which it was born. This time corresponds again to the First Station. The child eagerly explores the world around him or her outside the home, usually becomes either an avid reader or television watcher and is extremely receptive to the arts—music, painting, poetry and so on. The Personal Attribute of this Upper Wheel of Humanity is creativity. The Destiny is exploration.

Points 10, 11 (ages 9, 10)—Middle Wheel of Humanity. These are the years when the child begins to belong to groups and runs around with others of the same age and sex. Through this, the child achieves stabilization of what he or she has mastered so far, and this period corresponds to the emotional stabilization of the Second Station. The Personal Attribute of Points 10 and 11 is belonging. The Destiny is choices.

Points 12, 13, 14 (ages 11–13)—Pearl Drop of Humanity. Early puberty, represented by this period, is again highly important in revealing the status, life potential and longevity of the individual. The child develops tastes through choice of companions, clothes, music and heroes. It is an idealistic and often religious period, when belonging to a chosen social group becomes supremely important. Development and integration of emotional and cultural values make this period of the nature of the Third Station. The Personal Attribute of the Pearl Drop of Humanity is idealism; the Destiny is conditioning.

The Forehead Points

Points 15 to 30 (ages 14–29) are on the forehead, a feature representing character and comprising the First Station, indicating the beginning of the adventurous period of youth. These are the years of getting an education, separating from parents, establishing a family and career. This area represents the planet Mars, and its color should be pinkish.

Point 15 (age 14)—Mars (Fire Star). This point is in the hairline at the top middle of the forehead. Mars represents the Fire of Youth, and this floating year is a time when a youth takes responsibility for his or her sexuality, when the teenage revolt often is initiated as independence begins to be realized. It is the first year of adulthood, when identity is established and the first tests for control of the wild energies of youth are initiated. It often involves educational decisions (young people begin deciding on their majors at school) that affect later careers. For some, it is the time of their first encounter with the law and their decision of whether they will be on the side of the establishment or the rebels. Romantic overtures and sexual experiments are fantasized or attempted. All the fire and enthusiasm and adventure fostered by Mars come into play. The Personal Attribute of Point 15 is enthusiasm. Its Destiny is initiation.

Points 16, 17, 18, 19, in the middle of the upper forehead, are all growing-up points and represent the finding of identity and the separation from parents. Points 17 and 18 together are called Parent Points and represent how one treats one's parents (and consequently one's respect for oneself), and Points 16 and 19 represent the finding of one's own identity and acceptance as a grown-up. Both 16 and 19 are "middle points" and are extremely significant for the building of a constructive life pattern. (See also the 13 Middle Points.)

Point 16 (age 15)—Middle Sky. Though it is a middle point, this is a masculine, paternal (Yang) point concerned with the finding of identity. The mental element is strong, and one is concerned with planning a future career, developing tastes and desire for possessions and displaying responsibility that will lead to granting of greater privileges by the parents. The choice of companions is highly important in this year, because it is a time of deciding what the future will be like. Positive decisions can lead to success; negative decisions can lead to jail. Because it is a paternal point, the influence of the father as a role model or as a factor to rebel against is strong, and the resistance to authority (father, law, school, discipline) may also be strong. As it is a middle point, it concerns becoming your own person. The Personal Attribute of Point 16 is search. The Destiny is finding of identity.

Point 17 (age 16)—Sun Point. This is the Yang (paternal) Parent Point, when the relationship with the father is of paramount importance. Here you should resolve your conflict with your father (or dominant parent) and other authority figures—school, the law, your boss if you have taken a part-time job, for example. Because it is the year when most young people get a driver's license and either acquire a car or are allowed to use the family car, the establishment of responsibility to the family authority figure is significant. The way you treat your father as demonstrated in this year has much to do with your own self-respect and with your own role in the future as a parent. For many young people, this year represents a struggle between their own independent spirit and their dependency on others (father)—hence the first job, which gives some financial independence, or the first car, which gives social independence. It's also a time of physical and mental vigor, with opinions becoming shaped and athletic feats instilling self-confidence. For many, it is the year of sexual initiation; proof of sexual prowess and attractiveness often dominate. The Personal Attribute of Point 17 is vigor; its Destiny is responsibility.

Point 18 (age 17)—Moon Point. This Parent Point represents the mother and the development of the emotional, receptive Yin side of the nature, when the relationship with the Mother is of prime importance. Here you should resolve conflicts with the mother (or with the more passive parent) and develop the emotional and social side of your nature. This year is often concerned with whom you know and where you are accepted, with dating and the Yin (skin, flesh) side of your physical being. Physical attractiveness, the development of personality and the establishment of friendships gain attention; compassion and love dominate sexual and romantic adventures, and often young people become involved in social betterment and extend their social pleasures through group activities. The protective, maternal side of one's nature (as opposed to the authoritative, paternal side) develops, and often a true appreciation of one's parents becomes noticeable. The thing to be aware of in this year is how you treat your mother, for upon this will depend how much consideration you (male or female) will show to your mate and also how much pleasure you will derive from your own emotional nature in the future. The Personal Attribute of Point 18 is compassion. The Destiny is approval.

Point 19 (age 18)—Court of Heaven. This is another of the significant middle points, representing coming of age, making your entrance into society and being accepted as a grown-up. Though it is a middle point, it is a maternal, feminine point, complementary to Point 16, Middle Sky (paternal, masculine), the finding of identity. Traditionally in the West, this is the time of finishing prep or high school, of making social debuts and, for some young women, the age of marriage. For young men, it is the age of military registration and often for starting a full-time job. For many of both sexes, it is the time of leaving home for the first time—to go to a job, a family of one's own or college. This is the year when to a great extent you determine your life status; present decisions determine success. In China, it meant acceptance at court—a kind of debut into the world of grown-ups for the youth. You begin to be treated as an adult. In some states, you can buy liquor, get an adult driver's license, vote, get married without parental consent and be held responsible for your own debts and actions. What you should keep in mind this year is your future status. Attempt to meet and win favor from influential people, be respectful to those who can be helpful to you and show yourself as a person with potential. This applies predominantly on the social level; those who go to college will join clubs and other organizations that will affect their future for good or ill. Those who enter the work field make new associations. The Personal Attribute of Point 19 is flowering; its Destiny is social acceptance.

Points 20 and 21 (ages 19–20), taken together, are the Assistants, or Deputies. In these years, you are taking over responsibilities from your parents and learning from others by assisting them in their duties or carrying out their plans. For many, it is the period of preparation for career through education; for others, it is a period of apprenticeship at the job for future benefits. Assuming the role of assistant or deputy at this period is beneficial for your life work, and you should use it to gain knowledge and to further your future career.

Point 20 (age 19)—Deputy. This is the Yang, aggressive, masculine point in which you serve the authority figure as a representative and learn how the business is conducted. Or, if you are in school, you get the benefit of your teacher's knowledge and experience and carry out assignments. It is best this year to be in an outgoing capacity, encountering new experiences. But it is not a time when you should be greatly assertive and assume authority, though you can share ideas, make suggestions and expand your experience. You do best in the role of a deputy without too much responsibility except to carry out instructions. It is important to choose a boss or an instructor you can admire and use as a role model in your future enterprises, and also to get useful experience. This time shouldn't be wasted in a nothing job or in easy courses, because it represents an important stage in your development. The Personal Attribute of Point 20 is serving; the Destiny is experience.

Point 21 (age 20)—Assistant. This is the Yin or passive, accepting point at which you consolidate the experience of the previous year's apprenticeship or studies and gain control over your knowledge. In work or study, you carry out the instructions of your mentor and absorb knowledge from helping. Now you can determine what areas of your chosen field are likely to be best for you and weigh the emotional satisfactions you are likely to get from your career, along with the money and status that will come with it. Now you should accept the discipline of work, learn to carry out orders and stick to the job. Again, it isn't a good time to try to be in control. You are still in a period of learning. The Personal Attribute of Point 21 is following. The Destiny is obedience.

Point 22 (age 21)—Steward of Heaven. This represents the true coming of age, taking one's place in the world as a citizen. Again, this is a significant middle point. At age twenty-one, your ability to manage affairs and handle people will be tested. This may be on such an elemental level as managing your own budget and housing or taking on your own health insurance. In any event, you are now considered an adult and capable of taking charge of your own life. What concerns you this year is making your own decisions, handling your own affairs and dealing with people on your own as a grown-up. You also are wise to define your goals and learn to be a self-starter (if you haven't already). The Personal Attribute of Point 22 is capability. Its Destiny is independence.

Points 23 and 24 represent Lands that Lie to the Side. These points are concerned with travel, exploration of opportunities as well as new locations, moving in and out of business and social environments and getting experience of the world. They represent times when people change jobs and often locations, try out new fields of enterprise or travel extensively between finishing college and taking a job.

Point 23 (age 22)—The Fringe. This is the Yang point, representing travel for opportunity, changes in business and intellectual explorations. Usually this is the year you finish college, take a long trip or do something that will further enlarge your experience. You also explore new fields of thought and perhaps new lines of work—and may be sent by your firm to an outlying district. The important thing about this year (and the next) is not to tie yourself down too rigidly, to leave room to explore and move about and make changes before your career becomes fixed. Usually job changes made in this year will be beneficial, and as long as you keep your eye on your main goal, you will make out all right. Be aware that this point is on the paternal, aggressive Yang side of your face and that movement in a defined direction is encouraged. It's a time when you can take chances and expect good results; movement in anything makes for improvement. The Personal Attribute of this point is adventure. Its Destiny is movement.

Point 24 (age 23)—The Outskirts. This is the corresponding Yin point and indicates explorations through changing social environments and travel for pleasure, changes in relationships and trying out new contacts and social groups. Again, do not become too settled yet in your life plan. Consider where you want to go in your personal life as well as in your work, get to know more people, try new hobbies and activities and put yourself in contact with a variety of people before you settle for one partner or one social level.

If you can travel for pleasure and knowledge—a kind of grand tour before going to work—this is the year to do it. For some young men and women, ages twenty-two and twenty-three are when they do their military service, whether required or voluntary. Others who have aspirations in the arts may travel to a congenial place to practice their painting, music, film and so on. It's a fun year, one in which you can test yourself in a variety of ways and find your true being. The Personal Attribute of Point 24 is experiment; its Destiny is change.

Point 25 (age 24)—Center of Heaven. This is a significant middle point and indicates the time you assume control of your own destiny. This might be the year of your first starring role in whatever field you have chosen—marked by an outstanding job promotion, a publication or sale or ownership of your business, or the establishment of your own company or marriage and/or starting a family. This is a year when you make your first significant mark on the world and enjoy the first fruits of success. Your test this year will be how well you can handle people—if you have employees or helpers, how well you manage them; if you must meet others, how affable you can be; how much understanding of others you have and how well you read people. These are things to work on in this important year. If you marry, you will be tested in getting along with your mate and possibly your mate's whole family. Keep in mind all this year what effect you have on others and how this affects your success. The Personal Attribute of Point 25 is influence; its Destiny is triumph.

Points 26 and 27 are the Monument and the Mausoleum. They are actually travel points, not death points, perhaps because a chief reason for travel in ancient China was to visit the shrines of one's ancestors. However, they are in a sense concerned with your relationship to those who came before you and those who will come after you, as your life is affected by your background.

Point 26 (age 25)—The Monument. This is the positive, paternal, aggressive Yang point of the pair. It represents travel for discovery, perhaps to find a better location, perhaps to find new markets or new business or simply to enlarge your own horizons. Also, as the Monument, it indicates making a mark in the world, either through work that leaves an important heritage to society or by starting your own family (a good year to have a baby). It could mean the start of a political career or a new, important line of work. But it marks an achievement for which you will be remembered in the future. The Personal Attribute of Point 26 is brightness; its Destiny is a turning point.

Point 27 (age 26)—The Mausoleum. This is also a travel point, but the Yin, or emotional point of the two. The travel indicated will probably be for pleasure, for family matters or to explore the past, perhaps your own roots. This may also be the year in which you receive an inheritance. It indicates a time to evaluate the past, to explore your heritage and give respect to what your predecessors have brought to you. Travel now to visit family, to return to the place of origin of your family or to visit the old family home (if any) to give yourself a chance to assess your place in the scheme of things. Even if you travel only for pleasure and experience, you benefit. The Personal Attribute of Point 27 is reflection. Its Destiny is inheritance.

Point 28 (age 27)—Shrine of the Seal of Heaven. This is the most important point on the forehead, a middle point in a star-point area. This is the year in which you can achieve fame, true adulthood, self-responsibility—and the Seal of Approval. The point indicates success—you can star in worldly matters. But it also is a spiritual point, and for many, it initiates a renewal or finding of religious faith or some kind of spiritual blessing. In other words, you may think of yourself for this year as the darling of the gods and look for luck to follow your achievements and for supportive vibrations from higher powers. Now others begin to respect your abilities, and you get gratification for your own endeavors. In a sense, this is the high point of youth and will prove to be one of the most significant years in your life. The Personal Attribute of Point 28 is daring; its Destiny is good fortune.

Points 29 and 30 again are travel points and represent the searching and exploration that is characteristic of the transition period between youth and midlife.

Point 29 (age 28)—Mountain or Highland. At this age, you have reached a high point and now become aware of the ups and downs of life. Here you must put out more effort to maintain your position. This is a travel point, relating often to change and travel for escape from pressures or, sometimes, as an expression of competence, wealth and success. Business travel is common in this year, along with changes to a more opulent life-style or more influential social set—reaching higher on the upward scale. Some may see it only as a climb up the executive ladder; others as an elevation in status, others as reaching a higher emotional or spiritual plane. It is likely that travel to mountains and other high places will be appealing to you, and that you will incorporate tests of physical vigor into your trips, because you are still in an achieving situation. The Personal Attribute of Point 29 is moving upward; its Destiny is expression.

Point 30 (age 29)—The Forest. This is a travel point, and much of the travel done early in this year will be for escape and pleasure. But later, the travel will be done to find something you feel has been lost. This is a transition year—many people feel lost as they approach age thirty. The spiritual and emotional searching in this year is like Dante's wandering in the dark wood at the opening of *The Divine Comedy*. It is wandering in search of spiritual values—and you may feel lost in a dark wood before you find a clearing. There is a kind of restlessness about this year that must be turned into purposeful searching if you are to come out of it handily. This year also indicates a kind of return to innocence, as you reexperience some of your childhood fears and dependencies. One good way to handle this year is to realize that you pass from it into the brilliant star-point period, and that the emotional and psychological changes you experience now are strengthening you for that exciting development. It's a good time, too, to shed hang-ups and emerge as a new person. The Personal Attribute of Point 30 is wandering; its Destiny is transition.

Eye Area Points

At Point 31 (age 30), you enter the star-point area. You have already passed through one star point (Point 28, Purple Air). But through Points 31 to 41 (ages 30–40), you are at the shining part of your life. This will always be for you a period of special brilliance. The years in which your position points fall in this area are a time of achievement and reward as well as of personal development. You also at this time pass from the adventurous First Station to the stabilizing Second Station—the Mid-life Period.

The eyebrow points—Points 31 to 34—continue the development of the honors you received at Point 28, The Shrine of the Seal of Heaven.

Point 31 (age 30)—Floating Cloud. Point 31 is related to the left eyebrow—the Baron—and is a time of significance and importance, when you are much in the public eye and receive acclaim. Though age thirty is much maligned by those who have not yet reached this point, the experience of this year is much appreciated by those who leave themselves open to enjoy it. It is a lucky year, during which things are easy to achieve and efforts are speedily rewarded. Keep in mind that you are competent and are making your place in the world—you're entering the best years of your life. The Personal Attribute of this year is confidence. The Destiny of this point is recognition.

Point 32 (age 31)—Purple Air. Do not confuse this point with the Star Point Purple Air, which lies *between* the brows, though they both have the same name and both are concerned with fame and good fortune. This is the corresponding Yin point to Point 31 (Yang) and lies near the right eyebrow, the Counselor. This represents a period when you are walking on air—when you can accept the pleasures and perquisites of your recent achievement and recognition. Again, it is a year when things come easily— and when you should relax, enjoy yourself and get good advice. Consolidate your recent gains and accept your rewards. The Personal Attribute of this point is enjoyment. Its Destiny is satisfaction.

Points 33 and 34 (below the eyebrows) are together called the Rainbows. They represent a colorful part of your life and are associated with enlightenment and good fortune but also a reconsideration of your values, when you discriminate among the various opportunities life has to offer and decide on a future course.

Point 33 (age 32)—Colorful Rainbow. This represents a time when you separate the essential parts of life, as light is broken up into its components by a rainbow or prism. You are now required to discriminate and make choices, to define your values and sort out what you want and how you will go about getting it. This will be brought about by a variety of colorful experiences, by meetings with meaningful people, by the offering of many options that require choices and discernment. You will see beneath the surface of things and will perhaps at times be picky. You also refine your tastes in cultural areas and somehow come to know what you want out of life. The Personal Attribute of Point 33 is discernment. The Destiny of Point 33 is opportunity.

Point 34 (age 33)—Kaleidoscope of Color. This is the Yin point corresponding to the Yang point, 33. This is again a colorful year, with interesting events and people entering your life, but it is a time when you consolidate your values and viewpoint and form patterns for your future, as a kaleidoscope takes random bits of colors and integrates them into a pattern. Here you tend to define your interests in occupation and cultural areas and choose your friends and social patterns more discriminatingly. Often political and social attitudes become set at this time as you recognize where your own interests lie and associate yourself with like-minded people. Because this is happening to some extent, it is wise to keep your options open—to get to know many different kinds of people and try a variety of outlooks so you can be sure that you have a complete overview before you narrow your goals. The Personal Attribute of this point is selectivity. The Destiny is adjustment.

The six eye points—Points 35 to 40, representing the ages thirty-four to thirty-nine, should be considered as a unit and represent the big campaign of your life—the life project or energizing of the life experience. The eyes—each is a star point—represent inner energy and intelligence, the individual expression of the cosmic energy. The left eye is Sun Star, representing the positive Yang force. The right eye is Moon Star, representing the receptive Yin force. The position points of these years alternate between the positive and receptive forces, so that in one year, you initiate, and in the following year, you consolidate your gains. Keep in mind that you are in the star-point area and that this should be a brilliant stage of your life.

The focus of these years is not only upon one's life work but also upon one's inner growth and personal development.

Point 35 (age 34)—Yang. This point represents the positive, early stage of development in which projects are initiated and first steps are taken in the areas of achievement. This should be a brilliant year when you do not hesitate to make fresh starts, new beginnings, to find fresh personal expression and to widen your areas of expertise. The inner energy this year should be at its most positive strength. The Personal Attribute of this year is inner energy. The Destiny of this year is affirmation.

Point 36 (age 35)—Yin. This point represents the *receptive* early stage of development in which you consolidate the gains of efforts made at Point 35. This, too, should be a brilliant year when you test the ground you have already covered and shore up any weak spots. If you need extra training or knowledge to carry on your projects, seek it now. Also look for good advice. The Personal Attribute of this year is inner strength. The Destiny of this year is receptivity.

Point 37 (age 36)—Middle Yang. This positive middle stage of development is a growth period in which you undertake the maturing of the projects you have started in the last two years and in which you work constructively toward the success that you can hope to achieve. This is a brilliant year, when inner energy is strong and vitality is high. It should be a period of expansion of intelligence and the promotion and projection of your ideas and desires. The Personal Attribute of Point 37 is resoluteness. The Destiny of this position point is progress.

Point 38 (age 37)—Middle Yin. This is the receptive middle state of development, when you strengthen your position and consolidate your gains of the past year. Recognize that this is again a brilliant year, when you star. But it is a receptive period, when your inner energy is replenished and when you do better to let things come to you rather than to make positive efforts to extend your sphere of influence. In your personal growth, you tend to rely more on intuitive wisdom than on rational thought, and you are highly creative. The Personal Attribute of Point 38 is intuition. The Destiny of this position point is unfolding.

Point 39 (age 38)—Late Yang. This is the positive third stage of development. Now you begin to put the finishing touches on your work, enjoying the fattening of your harvest. You make positive efforts not so much to expand as to protect what you have so far built into your enterprise. You are preparing your fruits for the harvest. Keep in mind that this is again a brilliant year, when your success is assured and you are able to deal with most problems with little trouble. The Personal Attribute of this year is awareness. The Destiny of this year is increase.

Point 40 (age 39)—Late Yin. This receptive third stage of development is the time when you see the harvest of your efforts and can look with satisfaction at what you have achieved. You should make an effort now to avoid loss, to hold your achievements together in order to experience the fulfillment of what you have undertaken. This is again a brilliant year, when in your personal growth you achieve new insights into yourself and others and the meaning of your existence. The Personal Attribute of Point 40 is enlightenment. The Destiny of Point 40 is fulfillment.

Mid-Face Points

You emerge from your creative period to find yourself at age forty at Point 41—the Root of the Mountain. This is a significant middle point and also falls in the star-point area Moon Dust. The mountain in this case is the nose, and the Root of the Mountain begins the period of achievement and success and also the accumulation of wealth, which is the function of these middle years of ages forty to forty-nine. You will also be involved with other mountains—the cheekbones, East Mountain and West Mountain, which represent power. This period of practical achievement is a consequence of the creative period you have just been through.

Point 41 (age 40)—Root of the Mountain. This marks the beginning of life achievement and often is the indicator of success or failure in the practical world. It is concerned with possession, position and, through marriage, with those close to you and also with your safety in life. Bear in mind that this is also a year in which you can star. Often you have to make hard decisions and perhaps demands on others to establish your control. Do not hesitate to be somewhat hard-nosed in this year, because it is a time when your whole future success is determined, and much can be won or lost. In your personal life, strengthen relationships—especially your marriage relationship—and establish partnerships. Take care of even the littlest details this year, because you are beginning an ascent of the mountain, and any carelessness can be hazardous. Many people do become careless because they think they "have it made" at this point, when they are actually at a new beginning. The Personal Attribute of this year is family reunion. The Destiny of Point 41 is holding together.

Points 42 and 43 represent places and, in a sense, the acquiring of property. They are both years of pleasure and also of personal growth. They lie just below the inner corner of each eye.

Point 42 (age 41)—Delicate Cottage. This represents a place of seclusion and intimacy and also a time of retreat from the outer world for the development of the inner world. This is a year when you may buy a vacation home or seek a place of seclusion and when you will want to spend time in self-evaluation and introspection rather than forcing yourself upon others. It may be only that you will spend more time in your own company or in that of your family, but it should be a year of pleasure and rest. You are still in a star-point area and will be much sought after even in retreat. The Personal Attribute of this year is intimacy. The Destiny of this year is introspection.

Point 43 (age 42)—Bright Palace. This is a year for conviviality and self-expression. You will be around many people and will entertain and be entertained. You will seek out lively places and colorful people and enjoy luxurious surroundings. If you travel, you stay at the best hotels; if you entertain, you host brilliant people. As a guest, you enjoy dynamic friends. At this time, many people find they come of age socially as conversationalists and perhaps as entertainers. Fill your life with lots of light and color and music, and enjoy. The Personal Attribute of Point 43 is conviviality. The Destiny of this point is self-expression.

Points 44 and 45 (ages 43 and 44) are on the nose, which represents wealth, and both are concerned with the health and longevity that are necessary to establish wealth and success.

Point 44 (age 43)—Sitting on Top of One's Age. This is a health point, for many a time when they feel they are getting old, over the hill, so to speak, when actually they are still on their way to the peak. It is a good year to get a physical checkup, but also a time to start a diet or exercise regimen that will put you into a prime condition of physical vigor in order to keep you vital and strong for your achievements. At one time, this and the following year were considered the prime of life. And the designation of these points bears out the importance of health in success. The Personal Attribute of this year is stamina, and the Destiny of this year is vitality.

Point 45 (age 44)—Sitting on Top of One's Longevity. This is a point at which one begins to prepare to enjoy the fruits of old age, both by physical planning and also by economic planning for comforts in later life, and also a time when, in personal growth, one should establish the sports and hobbies that will be continuing interests as one goes along. Now you should consolidate your position in life and take safety precautions. The Personal Attribute of Point 45 is resourcefulness. Its Destiny is accumulation.

Points 46 and 47 are on the cheekbones, which represent power. So a power struggle of some kind often goes on now.

Point 46 (age 45)—The Summit. This is usually a time when those on the executive ladder achieve power and control over others. Also, you should establish self-control and determine where you want to be and how to get there. Do not step backward in this critical year but move ahead to gain control over as much as you can in the way of authority. This is the positive Yang power point. The Personal Attribute of this point is authority, and its Destiny is power over others.

Point 47 (age 46)—The Crest. This is the Yin receptive power point, and it usually represents the ability to resist others' gaining control over you and to hold onto the power you have, but not to assert new controls and try to take new territory. Consolidate the gains you made in the previous year, and in matters of habits, exert self-control. Control of negative habits (such as drinking, smoking, overeating) can be established now. The Personal Attribute of this point is resistance. Its Destiny is power over self.

The nose indicates wealth, and the tip of the nose, including the nostrils, holds the Palace of Wealth. The nose also represents the planet Saturn (Earth Star).

Point 48 (age 47)—Peak of Perfection. This is the Throne of the Emperor. It represents the high point of achievement in life. It is the point at which others look up to you, seeing you at the top, while you are looking down the other side. This year involves your wealth but also your personality and character; an evaluation of your whole life is in order. Having reached the peak, you can more or less decide whether it was worth it, review what you have achieved and where you failed as well as where you succeeded. This is a year to enjoy full-blown success and to hold ground but not to plan more expansive efforts in the future. Once you are on the peak, there is every temptation to go higher, but it is wise to sit, rocklike, and enjoy the fruits of your success. The Personal Attribute of this point is self-satisfaction; the Destiny of this point is success.

Point 49 (age 48)—Balcony. The left nostril on which this point falls is also known as the Platform or the Governor and represents civil or government officials. This is a year in life when you may decide to enter public office or become a community leader, an instructor or otherwise fulfill civic duties and responsibilities. The Balcony is a point from which you look out upon life. In your personal life, it is a good time to review your position and look out upon the remainder of your life and consider your contribution and how you can extend it. The Personal Attribute of the Balcony is looking ahead. The Destiny of this point is public service.

Point 50 (age 49)—Pagoda. The Pagoda is a landmark that is seen from a distance, but pagodas were built originally as military lookouts, and the right nostril, upon which this point falls, is also called the Lookout and represents military advisors. If you are in the military hierarchy, you could come to a high position at this time. Even if you are not, you may feel more militant at this period and will be likely to exert firmer discipline upon yourself and those around you—employees or family. It is a fine year to establish control and to accept accolades. People notice you this year, and you may be called upon to exercise power. The Personal Attribute of this point is militance. The Destiny of this point is acclaim.

Lower Face Points

It should be noted here that most people who live to enjoy the whole decade of the fifties usually consider it one of the most rewarding decades of life. It is a time of well-deserved pleasures, and many people are surprised by the youth and vitality they feel at this period, when members of the younger generation often think their elders are over the hill.

Point 51 (age 50)—Center of Life. This point falls on the philtrum, the groove that connects the nostrils and the upper lip, and which, as we shall see, has to do with productivity and the life force of sexuality. Productivity should be high, and though age fifty, like any year that begins a new decade, is often dreaded by those who approach it, this usually turns out to be a happy year. For one thing, sexuality is strong, and it often proves to be a year when, in Western culture, many men and women begin an affair or even start a new marriage. For the solidly married, it is a time when satisfactions are derived both from the marriage and the children. For many, it is the year of the first grandchild or other joyous result of reproductivity and the life force. The Personal Attribute of the point is sexuality. The Destiny of this point is productivity.

Points 52, 53, 54 and 55 along the upper lip relate to the storage areas of the court—and in one's own life and personality, to the things one has accumulated.

Point 52 (age 51)—Warehouse (place to store possessions, things to be kept). By this time in life, one has usually accumulated a lot of material possessions and may be wondering what to do with them and where to put anything new that comes into the household. It's a time when individuals are often house-proud and pleased with the outward signs of success, enjoying their bank accounts, fat portfolios, comfortable surroundings, cars and so on. Wisdom by this time has been acquired, too, and knowledge and one's store of information and experience is great. The Personal Attribute of this year is pride. Its Destiny is acquisitiveness.

Point 53 (age 52)—Storage Area (place of merchandise, things to be disposed of). This is a time when an individual has a lot to offer and can sell his or her experience, knowledge and position for a good salary and good income. It is also a time when people begin to sort out the things they want to keep and those they want to get rid of. Sometimes it is a time when a decision is made to leave the family home and move into a small apartment or otherwise get rid of the unwanted and consolidate one's ac-cumulations. It is a better time to sell than to buy. It is also a year when you can get rid of old hang-ups. The Personal Attribute of this point is evaluation. The Destiny is merchandising.

Point 54 (age 53)—Food Depot (place where the nutrients of life are stored). This is a time when you consider the nurturing of life, both in regulation of diet and sustenance and in considering what feeds the mind and soul as well as the body. The physical body that has stored its nutrients well has good bones, teeth and muscle and physical vitality. The well-nourished mind provides gratification. One is protected against famine physically and spiritually, and you also have acquired enough of value to sustain you against emergencies economically. The Personal Attribute of this point is nourishment. The Destiny of this point is providence.

Point 55 (age 54)—Strong Room (place where valuables are stored). Now you become aware of what is of value in your life— what is the true gold that you have accumulated through living— and also that you have acquired valuables that need to be kept in a strongbox. Now you must protect yourself against loss. The Personal Attribute of this point is vigilance. The Destiny of this point is protection.

Points 56 and 57 are on the laugh lines, a minor feature that has to do with longevity. In the imperial layout, these points represent the civil court and the military court, respectively. They are called Law and Order.

Point 56 (age 55)—Law. This point represents the civil courts—the law that maintains the social order. This is a time when you may be involved in a civil suit of some kind, but it is primarily, for the individual, the time when your conformity to the laws of nature will lead either to a long life or to your life being shortened. The natural law of life, if it is obeyed, should bring happiness (laughter) at this point and the prospect of a long and happy life ahead of you. The Personal Attribute of Point 56 is optimism. The Destiny of this point is justice.

Point 57 (age 56)—Order. This point represents the military courts or the keeping of order in society through the authorities. For the individual, it represents the prospect of long life through discipline and regulation of habits and the good defense of one's interests. The Personal Attribute of Point 57 is compliance. The Destiny of this point is regulation.

Points 58 and 59 are called the Tiger Tufts, because these areas sometimes develop folds (dewlaps) as one grows older and also because, in the plan of the court, they represent aides to military officials and to the civil officers of the courts who protect the community. These are the years when the tiger, the beast in you, is brought under control.

Point 58 (age 57)—Guardian. This is a year when your animal instincts are usually strong and are brought under control. There is a tendency to act rashly, sometimes to encounter pitfalls, to be accident-prone. It is a time when you may sometimes feel threatened by outside forces and overreact, or when inner urges become overpowering and you seek a last fling. It is certainly a time when you need to defend yourself and guard the inner and outer forces that may be disruptive. The Personal Attribute of this year is alertness. The Destiny of this Point is guardianship.

Point 59 (age 58)—Defender. This is a time when the tiger in you or threatening you is at last restrained. This is usually a ceremonious time, with a great deal of bravado and the calling up of forces to help you in your attack upon life. Again, you may be somewhat accident-prone, but you will also enjoy the challenges of this year. The Personal Attribute of Point 59 is bravado. The Destiny of this point is trophies.

Point 60 (age 59)—Mercury, the Water of Life. This significant middle point is also a planet point, and the planet is Mercury, Water Star, which has to do with emotions. The mouth itself as a feature represents personality. So this is a year when the personality and emotional life take precedence over material possessions and achievements, and you will feel a great deal of personal expansion. As this point precedes the decade of the sixties, when the happiness and comforts of maturity are most enjoyed, the personality and its attractions are your most effective tool in realizing the benefits of the coming years. This is a time to develop your personality and appeal to others and to exercise your charm. The Personal Attribute of this point is indulgence. The Destiny of this point is trust.

Point 61 (age 60)—Sea of Wine. This is another significant middle point. It represents the rewards and comforts of maturity—travel in comfort, good food, luxury; a time to drift around on your boat and relax with good companions and plenty of food and drink. Now many people discover the joys of maturity and the pleasures they have earned, and this is often one of the happiest years. Travel is gratifying, and there are chances to make new friends and acquaintances through moving around, dining out and other gourmet activities. The Personal Attribute of this point is enjoyment. Its Destiny is travel.

Points 62 and 63 (ages 61–62)—Cellars and Basements. These two years are concerned with the foundations underlying life, and in the plan of the court, they represent the underground compartments. These two years are spent in shoring up, if needed, the foundations of life and understanding the underlying structure of your existence. The Personal Attribute of these points is precaution. The Destiny of these points is support.

Points 64 and 65 (ages 63–64)—Pools of Water. These years are a time of contemplation, contentment, serenity and quiet pleasure, when you enjoy nature and the meaning of things and feel content with your achievement. The Personal Attribute of these points is contemplation. Their Destiny is serenity.

Points 66 and 67 (ages 65–66)—Golden Robes. This is the time of enjoying the honors and respect due you—the gold watches of retirement, along with the accolades and testimonials to your achievements, are often received here. The Personal Attribute of these points is well-being. The Destiny of these points is honors.

Points 68 and 69 (ages 67 and 68)—Return. These are "society points" and represent a time of lively conviviality and social experiences. Often people get in with a new crowd—postretirement—and spend a lot of time in reunions and social get-togethers, just enjoying themselves. The implication of *return* is a kind of second adolescence, a breakthrough to new ways of living or reviving old acquaintances, of doing things you haven't had time for and trying out new hobbies and entertainments. The Personal Attribute of Points 68 and 69 is sociability. Their Destiny is entertainment.

Point 70 (age 69)—Court of Justice. This is a balance point, and if you are ever to have good judgment and wisdom, you have it now. The Personal Attribute of this year is balance. The Destiny of this year is judgment.

Point 71 (age 70)—Buried Treasure. This is the last of the significant middle points and represents the finding of the "gold" of life, the buried treasure of the joys of a life well spent, the pleasures of the family and the wisdom you have acquired through your life. The Personal Attribute of this point is understanding. The Destiny of this point is riches.

Points 72–73 (ages 71–72)—Servants and Helpers. Now you need the help, the support of others. If you have managed your life well, you can depend on family, neighbors and friends and will be respected and admired. The Personal Attribute of these points is dependency. The Destiny of these points is management.

Points 74–75 (ages 73–74)—Status. These points represent the position you have reached in life, how you are regarded in your community by your family and friends and how satisfied you are with the position you have attained. What is said about you, written about you, what is lasting in the effect of your life—how many children and grandchildren, for example, are around to carry on your memory. The Personal Attribute of these points is remembrance. The Destiny of these points is veneration.

The Points 76 to 99, which run around the perimeter of the face, represent, in addition to the age points for the later years (ages 75–98), the twelve signs of the Chinese zodiac. The Chinese animal signs of the twelve divisions of the year correspond to the signs of the Western zodiac. For example, the Chinese New Year begins with the new moon in the Sign of the Dog, which corresponds to Aquarius (January 20–February 19). However, Chinese astrology is chiefly based on the twelve animal symbols in the pattern of twelve-year cycles, beginning with the Year of the Rat and ending with the Year of the Boar. To learn the animal symbol for the year you were born, look up your birth year in the table given in Appendix D. The numbers of the signs and their Personal Attribute and Destiny are given here.

Points 76 and 77—The Rat. The Year of the Rat produces people who are bright, clever, optimistic and never give up hope. They have fine character but tend to be meddlesome, like to get into different situations but are not thorough. Instead, they spread their talents around. The Personal Attribute of the Year of the Rat is cleverness. Its Destiny is hope.

Points 78–79—The Ox. The Year of the Ox produces leaders, strong-minded people who are also kind-hearted, but stubborn and not easily destroyed. They are calculating and careful, keeping to their own way and thinking things through, but temperamental if irked. Usually those born in the Year of the Ox are late bloomers more successful in old age. The Personal Attribute of the Year of the Ox is patience. Its Destiny is duration.

Points 80–81—The Tiger. People of the Year of the Tiger always come out winners at the end. They are quite careful, keep promises and always do what they say they will. Somewhat self-indulgent, they are also quite straightforward and aggressive—achievers—but a little dictatorial and strong-minded. They are independent and theoretical thinkers, with a liking for philosophy. Though they are very virtuous, they produce few offspring. The Personal Attribute of the Year of the Tiger is thought. Its Destiny is victory.

Points 82–83—The Hare. The Year of the Hare produces men and women who are graceful and artistic, more gentle than strong, who tend to make many friends and few enemies. The women are ladylike, the men, gentlemen. They are talkative, clever with words and basically dependable and loyal and are quick to show their feelings. The Personal Attribute of the Year of the Hare is gentleness. Its Destiny is rapport.

Points 84–85—The Dragon. Often the Dragon Year produces romantic dreamers. Dragon people like to do big things, to be leaders, but they do not want to bother about details and are careless of the needs of others. They are indulgent about pleasures and tend to be lazy. However, they have a creative spirit and high energy. The Personal Attribute of the Year of the Dragon is pleasure. Its Destiny is rulership.

Points 86–87—The Snake. Year of the Snake people are very artistic, creative and sensitive. They tend to be reserved and not too aggressive, but very nice and kind—very humane. Snake people tend to be introverted. They would rather take orders than give orders, and in any situation they tend to be sticklers, not easily diverted to anything else. They tend to be both slightly negative and slightly positive, so that it is difficult to be sure how they will react. Somehow, though they are hard to evaluate, they have a kind of inner knowledge and outer glow. Their Personal Attribute is charisma; their Destiny is higher mind.

Points 88–89—The Horse. Usually the Year of the Horse produces people who are bright, very pleasant and with an open, friendly character. But horse people are fighters, always wanting to be ahead and highly competitive. They can't keep secrets but still are friendly, diplomatic and get along well with others, being very talkative and sociable, tending to extravagance. Basically, however, they are positive people and always succeed. The Personal Attribute of the Year of the Horse is diplomacy. Its Destiny is display.

Points 90–91—The Ram. The Year of the Ram produces people who appear soft but are strong inside and usually very careful and alert. They do things carefully and see things clearly, have a sense of responsibility and are active in work. Because they are flexible, too, things usually work out for them somehow. It is considered more fortunate for men than for women to be born in this year. The Personal Attribute of the Ram is flexibility. Its Destiny is breakthrough.

Points 92–93—The Monkey. Usually people of the Year of the Monkey are wise and clever though somewhat too flexible and energetic. The men are strong; the women are those everyone listens to; both sexes like to be the boss, to dominate others. Both seek power and usually have a large number of children and bring them up nicely. The monkey is usually talented, good at details and sees things clearly. The Personal Attribute of the Monkey is curiosity. Its Destiny is dominance.

Points 94–95—The Cock. The Year of the Cock, or the Rooster, produces those who are intellectual and sophisticated and can predict things. They tend to work things out systematically and handle people well, being able to look at things clearly and put events into perspective. People of the Year of the Cock are very much involved in colors, in their home and their work. They are sociable and popular at parties and like to mingle with others. The Personal Attribute of the cock is sophistication. Its Destiny is perspective.

Points 96–97—The Dog. Basically, Year of the Dog people have a sense of responsibility and are truthful, loyal and friendly. They are good to their families and others, are active, have an attractive personality and pleasant emotional vibrations. Being bright and sensitive, they do unusual things in life—often becoming politicians and sometimes humorists. The Personal Attribute of the Year of the Dog is loyalty. Its Destiny is truth.

Points 98–99—The Boar. Year of the Boar people are nonconformists and like to go their own way, doing what they feel like. They are, however, strong-minded and energetic and can become leaders, though they are somewhat too self-centered and don't listen to others. The women are supersensitive and will be helpful to others and basically can become successful. The Personal Attribute of the Year of the Boar is self-will. Its Destiny is leadership.

Point 100—Completion. This represents the balance point of the cosmic energies Yin and Yang.

II

LIFE READING

THE THIRTEEN MIDDLE POINTS

Besides the position system—the 100 points of the floating year—professional Chinese face readers employ another, more complex system of 135 points. It consists of the 13 middle points and a varying number of adjacent points, totaling 135 on each side of the face. Only one side of the face is read, the other being considered a mirror image. With the 135 points, a complete life reading can be done, detailing the successes and failures, hazards and fortunes, marriages and offspring and the changing state of the individual throughout the life span. This complete life reading should be left to the professional, because most of us lack the time and the desire to master its details. However, a simplified life reading can be done by reading the 13 middle points—those running down the face. This will enable you to "stage your life" as to its high and low points and its expansion and outcome, and to prepare yourself for successes and hardships, along with improving your lot by inner change and foresight.

The thirteen middle points of the face—16, 19, 22, 25, 28, 41, 44, 45, 48, 51, 60, 61, 71—are the most significant points because they represent the highlights and changes in your life that add up to achievement and satisfaction or frustration and debility.

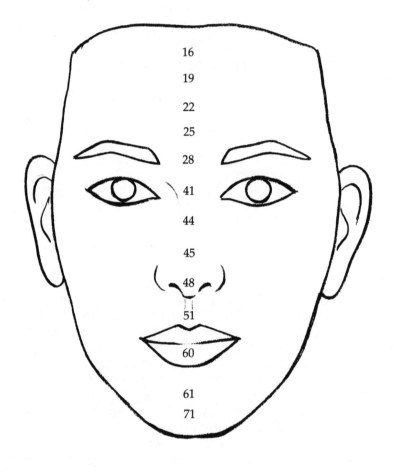

16

19

22

25

28

41

44

45

48

51

60

61

71

The good fortune they promise can alert you to prepare in advance for the advantages a particular period may offer. Any indicated hazards can be an incentive to correct your inner balance and mobilize your resources to minimize any misfortune and to help you guard against ill effects. They certainly can motivate you to positive changes to eliminate or at least ameliorate any ill effects you court through life-style and attitudes. Points 44 and 45—Sitting on Top of One's Age and Sitting on Top of One's Longevity—and Point 61—the Sea of Wine (or Pulp)—are, as we shall see, particularly amenable to the harmonizing effects of self-correction. And Point 60—the mouth, the Water of Life—is a feature we almost create ourselves by our attitudes and habits.

The color of these points—their glow and brightness or their discoloration or pallor—is also, according to the ancients, a guide at any time to vitality or ill health and can even warn of specific dangers—drowning, fire, robbers, the law. Keep a daily watch on the color of these points (see also the calendar of the face, pages 233–235), and be alerted by any changes. Although you may be dubious about the color of your nose as a guide to attack by robbers, it is, at any rate, a guide to your vulnerability to or immunity from life's ills.

1. SUCCESS IN YOUTH

The forehead points indicate success and vitality in youth, but this in itself is a preparation for success and vitality in the middle years. Even if the forehead points are not too promising of early achievements, the period they represent should not be idled away, because youth's problems, as well as its fortunes, prepare you for success in middle years and for security and health in old age. Likewise, if these youth points are the heights of your life, you should not expect to be washed out at thirty. In fact, youthful achievements are beneficial over the rest of your life.

Point 16—Middle Sky. If it is rounded (not flat) and clear, without lines or discoloration, it indicates one who achieves a lofty position early in life. It is a sign of high intelligence. Its owner travels, conquers many territories, makes lots of money—and all at an early age (before thirty). If there is a bony protuberance at this point, the individual is outstanding—a genius or a saint—and achieves high prestige and a tremendously elevated position.

If this area is flat or the color not good, or if it is lined or otherwise marked, you may never own land or property.

If this area is smooth, you will never be arrested.

Color: The forehead represents the Fire Star, Mars, and its color is red. So this and all the forehead points benefit when the color is bright, pinkish, and serve as a warning when the color is too whitish or dark or greenish. If this point is flat or marked to begin with and the color is not good, you may wind up in jail or may otherwise lose privileges.

Point 19—Court of Heaven. If the bone structure stands out here, particularly if there is a bony column rising up through Point 16, you are destined for a high position. The more prominent the bone here, the better. If this point is supported by points 17 and 18 (Moon Point and Sun Point)—meaning that the bone is protruding and not flat at these points as well—you can become known throughout the country and achieve a place of honor, becoming a cabinet officer or gaining other dignity.

If Point 19 is hollow or dented, it is very hard to become successful early in life. If this point is flat and smooth, you can achieve moderate success.

Color: Again, the color should be bright and pink. When it is bright and pink, you can change jobs for the better. If this point appears greenish, it indicates an unfortunate work situation.

Point 22—Steward of Heaven. This point is less significant than the previous ones, but if it is high, round and smooth, you can rise to an important managerial position and will do well as an executive. Many lines here make life difficult.

Color: Important are good color and smoothness. Pinkish brightness is helpful for a rise in position. Poor coloring indicates frightening experiences.

Point 25—Center of Heaven. If this area is round, smooth and unlined, you can rise in any field you enter.

Color: The color is bright and pink for employment success. When this point is white or discolored, you may be job-hunting.

Point 28—Shrine of the Seal of Heaven. This is a very important point: It is the point at which people see you. It reveals what your heart is like. Here you receive the seal—the stamp of approval. If it is smooth and bright, with no lines and good color; if the eyebrows don't grow into it; and if it has a kind of clarity and light, you are a darling of destiny. Age twenty-seven is the end of youth—the start of maturity—and your future is more or less settled at this time. It is wise to keep this point clear.

Color: The appropriate color here is clear, light and pink. If the color is dark, greenish or very white, and if there are lines in this area, it indicates problems—vulnerability to accidents, family problems, no peace.

2. SUCCESS IN MIDDLE YEARS

The promise of the middle years is not only for wealth and achievement, but also for health and longevity, so that you have the ability and time to enjoy your benefits.

Point 41—Root of the Mountain. This area is best when it is smooth and rounded, not flat and recessed. It is preferably clear of lines. Lines here create problems for your family. They also weaken health and reduce your potential.

Color: should be clear and bright. Poor color—dark, greenish— indicates that you lose money at age forty.

Point 44—Sitting on Top of One's Age. This area should be almost smooth, without a prominent bone. The bone should be smooth and straight and firm but with a good covering of flesh. This means your middle years will be stable, with no serious illnesses.

If the nose here is bony but not straight, with a bump, it can indicate health problems that may interfere with success in the middle years.

Color: The color of the nose is golden tan. Dark spots or greenish color create major problems. If this area is white and bleached-looking, someone in your family may be vulnerable to a serious illness.

Point 45—Sitting on Top of One's Longevity. The nose here is best straight, round and smooth to promise a long life.

If it is flat here, it shortens life expectancy.

Color: A golden tan color is healthy. A greenish tone shortens life by indicating an illness potential. Whiteness here creates problems in the family.

Point 48—Peak of Perfection. This point decides your potential for wealth. If it is round and smooth, you will possess riches. If it is round and straight, you are benevolent. If it is very pointed, you can be shrewd, ruthless and uncaring, and this creates problems for your spouse.

Thin and tiny: you cannot accumulate possessions. With a hook at the tip, you can be shrewd and scheming. Too rounded and too big: you may lack discipline, be too easygoing.

Color: The color of the nose should be tawny. If it is white, you can have problems in swimming, and may be in danger of drowning. Purplish color promises children. Red indicates robberies and fires.

3. SUCCESS IN LATER YEARS

The points of the lower part of the face are those most subject to change—for better or worse—by the life-style of the preceding periods.

Point 51—Center of Life. This point, the philtrum, is connected with reproduction and also has indications for the life span. The philtrum is the sewage system of the face and should be shaped like a canal, deep and straight and long, from the nostrils to the upper lip. In an average-size face, one inch is the ideal length. A long, well-formed, deep philtrum, smooth and without lines, indicates that you will maintain erotic activity well into old age.

Color: The philtrum should be the appropriate color for the element of the face. If it is too white, it indicates systemic poisoning. If it is too dark, it presages accidents.

Point 60—Mercury, Water of Life. The lips should be full, the mouth wide, with clear, distinct corners that turn up; the color should be reddish, and the mouth should appear moist. The mouth can never be too large (it is sometimes said that the mouth should be large enough so that you can almost put your fist into it) so long as it closes well and is not flabby. This kind of mouth indicates integrity and personality and well-being in old age. If you have this kind of mouth, you can be successful at whatever you do and enjoy a good constitution and a trustworthy nature.

If the mouth is thin and crooked, its owner is not to be trusted. If the corners turn up, there will be a good life with plenty of good fortune. If the corners turn down, you never seem to have enough. No matter how much you have, you want more. A large face with a small mouth shows poor position and little success.

The shape of the mouth is pretty much determined by how one lives and what one is. This is one of the easiest features to improve by achieving inner "rightness," so you will enjoy integrity and satisfaction in old age.

Color: The mouth should be red and moist. If it is dry and pale, it shows a lack of vitality.

Point 61—Sea of Wine. This area, if smooth and full, shows a pleasant, sociable person who travels and meets people and lives a colorful life. This applies throughout the life span, not only in old age. The owner of a full Sea of Wine is sociable, with a love of parties, enjoying many guests.

Color: The color should be yellowish gold, slightly pinkish. If the color is dark, the person should be very careful of drinking, because in the sixties, early overindulgence begins to take its toll.

If it is greenish or white, it indicates a fear of water or danger in water.

Point 71—Buried Treasure. This indicates the fruits enjoyed in old age. The chin should be clear and smooth, slightly squared and like a knob, not flat. This promises possession of property and land and having people to take care of you in your advanced years. The chin should be thick and slightly squared, not sharp. If it is sharp and thin, you will have no one to take care of you in your later years; no one will bother with you.

GUIDELINES

The thirteen middle points show the course of your life and the direction you will take. They also pinpoint the periods in your life when you will thrive and when you will have problems. Gratifying as it is to have a good beginning, it is especially satisfying to have successful middle years and to end up with a healthy and vital old age. By studying the middle points, you can begin to stage your life and set up your goals.

PART THREE

THE FIVE MAJOR FEATURES

POTENTIALS FOR ACHIEVEMENT

The Chinese see the face as composed of Five Major Features—ears, eyebrows, eyes, nose and mouth—and Seven Minor, or Compelling, Features—forehead, cheekbones, jawbones, chin, philtrum (the groove from the nose to the upper lip), undereye area, smile lines around the mouth. (Other features of the face—hairline, pattern of beard growth, eye and forehead lines, moles and so on also have meaning, but are not rated among the major or minor groups.)

The major features represent potentials for achievement, qualities you can develop in your life. The minor, or compelling, features represent the range or the limitations destiny imposes upon your achievement, factors over which you have little control.

Some of the features, as we have seen, are described as mountains and rivers. Among the major features, the ears, mouth and eyes are rivers.

The nose is in a sense both a mountain and a river, for the nostrils are rivers (moisture-producing), while the nose itself is the most prominent mountain of the face. Its tip is the Peak of Perfection—the Throne of the Emperor. The nose should be supported by the other mountains (the cheekbones, chin and forehead) but not crowded by them.

Each of the Five Major Features also represents either a planet or is a star point, and of those representing planets, each has its characteristic appropriate color. Certain of these features also represent body organs and so indicate health and vitality as well as personal characteristics and potential.

Look at the individual feature to find the nature of your own or another's potential in the area of life the feature represents. However, bear in mind that the potency of a feature can be supported or diminished by other features of the face. Examine each feature individually, and when you have done this, again consider the face as a whole. In Chinese face reading, balance and harmony are the desirable characteristics for a full, happy life. Also consider the inner glow, which can make any assortment of features appear harmonious.

Keep in mind, too, that no feature should be considered good or bad but only positive or negative for the characteristics this feature denotes. For example, long earlobes and big ears are beneficial for wisdom but not necessarily for good looks. The eyebrows represent fame, and for show business or other public enterprises, they should be prominent. Yet many successful people work behind the scenes without notoriety. Once you are aware of the inclinations the individual features promise, you can exploit or modify your practices to take advantage of their promise or to overcome their deficiencies.

In considering another's features, take into account the person's goals as indicated by the elemental type. Qualities needed for success in showmanship and finance would be different from those needed by a lawyer or actor, for example.

When you are considering the features, recognize that the use of the term *ideal* is a description of the form of the feature that is most effective in achieving its potential. And recognize what the ancient Chinese considered the greatest good: A long life with a happy old age; many children, grandchildren and great grandchildren; and money without having to work hard for it.

The ancient Chinese said that one positive feature will give you ten happy years, while five negative features can reverse and become an asset. An example of this is the Five Exposures. They are:

- back of ears exposed (ears bend forward)
- eyes exposed (protruding eyes)
- nostrils exposed (short or upturned nose)
- teeth exposed (short upper lip so teeth show even when mouth is in repose)
- underside of chin exposed (receding chin)

If you have all five, you are fortunate and can become rich if not wealthy. If, however, you have only one exposure (or any number fewer than five), this is considered unfortunate for the endowments you expect from the feature(s) involved.

The potentials represented by the Five Major Features are:

> ears—life potential
> eyebrows—fame
> eyes—intelligence, inner energy
> nose—wealth, achievement in mid-life
> mouth—personality

Begin your observation of the features with the ears, because they show the entire life potential in capsule form. Then go on to the other features one by one.

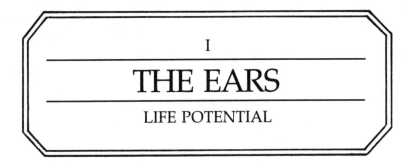

I

THE EARS

LIFE POTENTIAL

The ears, as a major feature, represent life potential. As we have seen, the ears are planet points. The right ear represents Jupiter, Wood Star, whose Vitality is rising and whose Fortune is wisdom. The left ear represents Venus, Gold Star, whose Vitality is grace and whose Fortune is status. The floating years of conception to age thirteen (Position Points 1 to 14) are represented by the ears. Position points 1 to 7 are on the left ear. Position points 8 to 14 are on the right ear.

You can, in fact, learn the entire life potential of an individual from the ears alone, for, although the ears represent the years of infancy and childhood, they fall in the Second Station, the part of the face that represents mid-life. And it is in the middle years that the influences of childhood—the care and nutrition of the child as well as its education and family background—bear most heavily upon the ability of the individual to achieve success both in work and in family life and to enjoy the good health and stamina needed to survive the tests of living.

When you observe the ears of another, visualize the kind of infant and child they suggest. This helps reveal adult tendencies. For example, a fleshy, overindulged child often becomes a self-indulgent adult; a wiry, hyperactive child may become a frivolous grown-up.

Bear in mind that the planetary color of the ears is white, and that they should always be lighter than the face, whatever the complexion color. The ears also are rivers, in that they produce moisture (ear wax). They should not appear too dry and flaky or too red and dark.

Among the body organs, the ears represent the kidneys. The function of the kidneys is to remove waste matter from the blood and also to help maintain the balance in body fluids, removing excess water and waste chemicals into the urinary canals. The color and moistness of the ears can thus reveal, according to Chinese face reading, how well the kidneys are functioning and hence the temperament and disposition of an individual. If the tissues are water-logged, one may become lethargic, phlegmatic.

Although professional face readers analyze the ears in great detail, we can study them according to their positioning on the head—high, medium or low—how close they are set to the head and by categorizing them as to their basic ear type.

Position. The position of the ears has much to do with the position in life.

High   Medium   Low

High-positioned ears. If the ears are set high, so that the top of the ear reaches above the top of the eyebrows, it shows one who is an early achiever and very intelligent and who will reach a high position in life at an early age. These ears actually rise above the Second Station into the First Station (youth) and thus show a life potential that demonstrates itself in the years before thirty. If these ears are also long, reaching down into the Third Station, the achievement of youth will be enduring into the later years.

Middle-positioned ears. If the ears have a medium placement, with the tops of the ears rising only to the space between the tip of the eyebrow and the outer corner of the eye, they carry the promise of success—in fact, their owner will be among the world's most successful people. He or she is destined to do well in business, can carry responsibilities ably and has the initiative to make a place in the world. Success often comes by one's own efforts and is reached in the middle years (Second Station). If these ears extend down into the Third Station (below the bottom of the nose), this success will carry over into the later years and also assure wise provision for the later years.

Low placement. If ears are placed low, so that the top of the ear extends only to the level of the outer tip of the eye or lower, it indicates one who perhaps makes little effort in life and is happy to have others do the work. A man with such an ear setting will often let his wife support him. A woman with such an ear setting does not care for a career and is willing to be dependent on her mate or, later in life, on her children. If, however, these ears are large, well formed and nicely set and are long enough to extend below the bottom of the nose into the Third Station, it indicates achievement late in life and a willingness to work in earlier years for a deferred benefit.

Set. You should also observe how close to the head the ears are set. The ears are best set close enough to the head so that the back of the ear is not exposed, but on the other hand, not so tight that they press against the skull.

Close-set ears. Close-set ears indicate prudence in the management of life but at the same time enterprise and wisdom in the handling of various factors demanded by the life potential. Again, much depends on the size, shape and position, but well-shaped, large ears set close are an asset.

Protruding ears. People with these ears are considered easygoing, somewhat irresponsible and inclined to lose things, and perhaps sexually promiscuous. Protruding ears that are also floppy are a sign of irresponsibility to self as well as to others. Protrusion that exposes the backs of the ears creates one of the Five Exposures, and if this is the only exposure, or if the person lacks one of the other five, it is considered unfortunate especially in money matters.

Tight-set ears. If ears are set tightly to the head, it indicates one who is overly cautious and who diminishes life potential by lack of the daring demanded for a successful existence. Such a person may be deficient in the adventurous spirit needed to rise to a high status and the wisdom to participate fully in life. The position of the ears and their basic type are also factors to consider in evaluating such tight-set ears, but unless they are large and well-formed, the foregoing applies. If tight-set ears are also thin and small, it indicates stinginess, a lack of pleasure in life and uptightness in the personality.

1. BASIC EAR TYPES

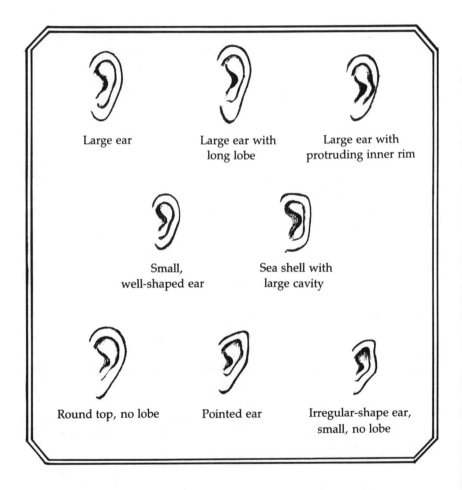

Large ear

Large ear with
long lobe

Large ear with
protruding inner rim

Small,
well-shaped ear

Sea shell with
large cavity

Round top, no lobe

Pointed ear

Irregular-shape ear,
small, no lobe

There are seven basic ear types, and most of the ears you observe (perhaps your own) will be among these types. There are, however, four special ears that are identified with animal types. Evaluate each ear in the context of its position and set as well as its basic type.

Large Ear—The Achiever

A large ear is an asset, especially if it is well formed and well positioned on the head. It indicates a strong life potential—a good character; a happy childhood; long, fruitful life. It is the ear of the successful businessman or businesswoman, a person whose providence and enterprise persist over a long period of the life span. Large ears indicate a person who has *large* ideas and sees matters as a whole, and whose enterprise continues, because the ears extend into the Third Station (last third) of the face. The large-eared person listens—catches the whispers and whimpers of life as well as the sonic booms—and is usually generous and compassionate, adding to his or her own worth and also building support for others through sound ideas and good deeds. Large ears are particularly helpful for women in business on their own, because they need the force and wisdom this kind of ear gives and have to keep an ear out, so to speak, for advantages. When you find this ear in a man or woman, you find a successful person who also is outgoing and aware and combines business acumen with goodwill.

Large Ear with Long Lobe—The Wise

To the qualities of the large ear, the long lobe adds deep wisdom, a growing philosophy of life and the opportunity for a long, fruitful life. This ear's owner is more likely to be in a profession—law, government, education, journalism, religion—than in the business world, and success is somewhat delayed in achievement, perhaps till the last third of life. But this person gets increasing respect and has influence in the later years, possibly becoming the leader of an influential circle of followers, someone who will be quoted, honored and listened to in old age. If the lobe is extremely long, it is called a Buddha ear, indicating spiritual as well as philosophical wisdom, and we can often benefit by listening to what such a person will have to tell us. This, again, indicates a person who listens as well as speaks and who may indeed be the mastermind of a generation. Note the other qualities of such an ear—position, set and color—because the wise may also be misleading to the young, and with poor other qualities, the owner of this ear can sometimes become a false prophet.

 ## Large Ear with Protruding Inner Rim— The Sophisticate

With such an ear, the individual is likely to be a nonconformist. Such people often are found to live far from their place of origin. They are adventurers, extremely sociable, interested in color, sound and effect and often lead colorful lives. They succeed in business if it is involved with social activities, if they can be in business for themselves and can be creative, even daring, about what they do. They forever look for new people, new ideas, new fads and want a chance to express their views and to speak out for any cause that attracts them at the moment. Basically, though, they are successful, and because of determination and influential friends, they can make a mark for themselves in the world. You find these people in sales, advertising, the arts, offbeat merchandising and fashion design rather than in manufacturing or the professions, which are too tame for them. These usually are very sophisticated, worldly people who like to live in cities, especially big cities, or in foreign countries. Note that these people like to go their own way. They may not be too reliable or secure. They want to take chances, but on their own, not depending on others, and often they will use and then drop those who have been helpful to them. Don't rely on their promises too much or depend on them to support your cause.

Small, Well-Shaped Ear—The Conformist

Usually this small, shapely ear is also set close to head. If so, it indicates one who is a conformist, well nurtured, well cared for and secure, extremely competent and well organized, who seeks stability and support from others in a well-controlled environment. Usually this person is graceful and artistic, a lover of color, with good taste and clearly defined goals. Success is often achieved in the middle years and may be in the field of decorating or the more conventional arts. Usually the person is a lover of sound as well as color, and good manners make it possible for these people to get obedience and service from others. Nevertheless, they are often demanding of perfection and order. Personal relationships are usually warm and become more stable as the individual grows older. There is a need for exquisite beauty and comfort in the environment—a good address, a pleasant view, traditional furnishings. Because of the love of tradition and the need for stability, this person may become inflexible in later years and may find it hard to adjust to change. Thus, he or she may be left behind by the world as he or she grows older. Fortunately, this small, competent ear makes it possible to secure one's future, and such people often live well even if they don't like the world they live in and want a return to the values of their youth. This small ear does not indicate a longer-than-normal life span, but the average length of life is well within their grasp. Depending on the setting of the ear, these people can reach a high or middle position or will be content with a lower echelon if they can express their tastes and competence.

Shell Ear with Large Cavity—The Open-Minded

This is the ear of the very outgoing, open-minded individual who hears everything, tells all and is happy only in the company of others. These people can be very successful, depending on how the ear is set, although they cannot expect to live beyond the normal life span unless other factors so indicate. Their success usually occurs in the sociable, voluble professions— merchandising, sales, running showrooms, galleries, catering, managing restaurants and hotels, social-club organizers—where they can be involved with others constantly and also can hear all the gossip. If this ear is thin and not well fleshed but strong, with good shape, the individual may become successful but is rather shallow and superficial. All in all, this ear produces someone who is a good host or hostess and who usually lives in comfortable and somewhat ostentatious surroundings, a person who is very much into day-to-day events but does not think a lot about the future and has great interest in new styles of living, changing with the popular views of things.

Round Top, No Lobe—The Idealist

This indicates one who is idealistic, has a good family background and is often lucky because of a tendency to be in touch with the ups and downs of the economy and of everyday life. Thus, this individual can easily adjust and take advantage of change. This is usually a happy person, and personal relations are usually smooth because of this individual's flexibility and compassion. But these people have short-lived success and will often find disappointment if they plan too much on future security. The lack of a lobe gives them only a normal life span, and it also denies them some of the wisdom that foresees future problems so they can be averted. This is not a thinker's ear, but it is a cheerful ear. Often its owner is well brought up, has a good family and makes influential friends—even if friendships, like other things, are not long-lasting—there is always someone new in their lives, just because they are so pleasant to be around. Opportunities often come without seeking, and these are people who fall into their work rather than have definite goals. Usually this means they work for others and they do not go into long-term fields, such as the professions or businesses that require a long haul up the executive ladder. Photographic models—male and female—have such ears; so do salespeople and those in merchandising who meet the public, such as demonstrators, buyers and salespeople in department stores. Also, areas of show business that don't require a great deal of fortitude and training are suitable for those with this ear. You also find this ear in the helping professions, because of youthful idealism and the wish to be of service to others. Success, however, often will not last beyond the middle years. This can mean dependency late in life, but these cheerful, well-meaning and generally optimistic people usually can find friends and helpers at any time in life.

Pointed Ear—The Opportunist

If the ear has a pointed top, it indicates a fun-loving person who is shrewd and impulsive, a bit of an opportunist, but one who is also fickle and somewhat of a drifter. This ear was associated in Greek mythology with the faun—half-man, half-goat, the seducer of nymphs, the plaything of the woods. People with this ear, however, tend to have charm, are fun to be around and enjoy life even if they are not dependable. If the ear is fairly large and has a lobe, the individual is more likely to be somewhat reliable and to be clever as well as shrewd and more purposeful in life, settling down somewhat in later years. If there is no lobe, the individual may become a drifter and have a short, if active, life.

People with pointed ears tend to go into occupations where they can take chances and sometimes where they can take advantage of others. Most people consider this ear untrustworthy, so you do not find its owners employed as cashiers or in banks or elsewhere where they need to handle money. They do, however, like to be around gambling establishments, racing, merchandising places where there is a quick turnover, in jobs where they can have fun without too much responsibility. Often they are trying to make good deals and fast money. But they also are clever and capable of success, especially early in life, and may be inventive and creative as well. People with this ear quickly "get the point" in any transaction and can come up with clever, quick ways to solve problems and get out of difficulties. In human relationships, they are, however, not reliable and often change partners and friends.

Irregular-Shape Ear, Small, No Lobe—The Misfit

Note whether this is a natural ear or has been deformed by accident or surgery. If it is natural, it indicates someone who gets a poor start in life, perhaps comes from a broken home and is restless, unreliable and always moving from place to place and job to job. Consequently, it is hard to establish a good position in life or much economic security. Thus, such a person may have problems forming relationships; often the individual is basically unstable and does not seek lasting contacts. It is important with this ear to note if other features of the face bear out the unreliability or whether the individual has compensating features that indicate more staying power, warmth and status in life than the ear promises. A short life is often indicated by this ear, because the person tends to live dangerously and often does not properly nourish the body, the mind or spirit to create a viable organism. Childhood problems are often a factor in the reckless living engaged in during adolescence, the middle years or later in life, if indeed the individual survives so long.

2. ANIMAL-TYPE EARS

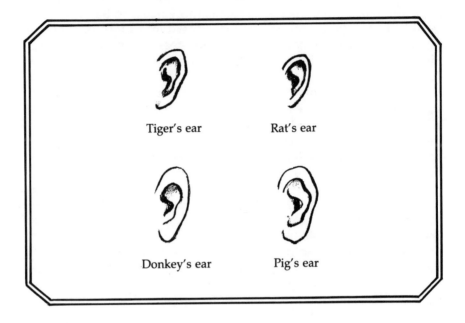

Tiger's ear   Rat's ear

Donkey's ear   Pig's ear

Some ears are associated with animal types. These ears are not usually signs of productive people and may possibly represent poor life potential unless other features redeem their poor auspices, or unless the individual is a *pure* animal type, with other features corresponding to the same animal.

Tiger's Ears. These are small and sharp in shape, with the wheels uneven, not smooth and curved. The owner of these ears may be successful but cannot sustain the success. The person may be too shrewd and deceitful and not kind-hearted enough to get the support needed for sustained success.

Rat's Ears. These are small, pointed ears and indicate one who may prove untrustworthy.

Donkey Ears. These ears are large and protruding and their shape is not good, for they are soft as well and tend to be floppy. These ears indicate a hard life with little achievement and poor chance of long survival in some circumstances; in other conditions, this person can make money.

Pig's Ears. These ears are large, with irregular shape and somewhat indefinite contour, because the texture is soft and the ears appear flabby. If other features are good, the person may do well, but basically these ears indicate bad luck, and their owner is often foolhardy and prone to have accidents.

GUIDELINES

The positive qualities in ears are large size, good shape, long lobes, set close to the head, with good position, reaching up at least to the area above the outer tip of the eye. Deformities in the shape of the ear, sticking out from the head, low position and especially poor texture (flabbiness or floppiness) indicate that the individual got off to a poor start in life, either through poor inheritance, a deprived childhood or a broken home. Look to other features for redeeming qualities.

The ears, representing life potential, give you an overview of the qualities inherent in the individual you are observing. Of the remaining four major features, each represents an aspect of this potential that can be developed and used in shaping the life.

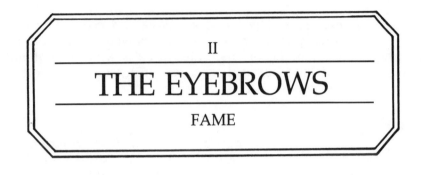

II

THE EYEBROWS

FAME

The eyebrows represent the claim to fame, reputation and area of achievement—ambitions, goals and the temperament that indicates possible accomplishment. The eyebrows, as we have seen, are star points—the left brow is the Baron, or Overlord, and the right brow is the Counselor. Ideally, the brows should be identical in shape and size. This means you have authority (the Baron) balanced by the wisdom (the Counselor) to use the authority prudently. However, in some faces, you will note a difference between the left eyebrow and the right eyebrow. Such a situation indicates that the individual will be rash in the use of authority (Baron dominant) or too cautious to use authority boldly (Counselor dominant).

Another point to note is that the brows are "violent stars" and should not intrude into other star-point areas. This chiefly means they should not meet above the nose, invading the Star Point Purple Air and also confronting each other in the other's territory.

The eyebrows mark the transition from the First Station (youth) to the Second Station (mid-life). Position Points 31 and 32 (Purple Air and Floating Cloud) and 33 and 34 (the Rainbows) are in the eyebrow area, showing the surge into success and discrimination that usually takes place in the early thirties. One's position in life then becomes clear, and it is a period when one is likely to come before the public.

It is extremely important for those who wish to achieve fame in the theater, the arts, showmanship, politics—anything that brings them before the public—to have distinctive and prominent eyebrows. However, personal reputation and good name are significant to all of us, and so the eyebrows in a way tell how each of us is judged by the outside world.

Here are general indicators of personality type found in the eyebrows, whatever their basic shape:

- Dark and heavy brows indicate one who is domineering and effective.
- Thin, light brows show one who is adaptable and amenable in public relationships—in a male, one who is likely to be a ladies' man; in either sex, a swinger.
- Long hairs within the brow after age 40 show a long life. However, light, shaggy brows with unruly hairs that stick up are an indicator of sexual promiscuity.
- Hairs in the outer tip of the brow pointing upward indicate help from friends.
- Smooth, well-shaped brows indicate controlled emotions, sexual fidelity and pleasant human relationships.
- A prominent bone beneath the eyebrows is considered fortunate and indicates fame that is of a noble nature rather than through notoriety.

The Ideal Brow. The ideal brow—ideal for a good name achieved through wise use of authority—is long and elegant, smooth and delicately arched, slightly wider at the inner tip but preferably almost all the same width or thickness between the inner tip (nearest the nose) to the height of the arch and tapering only slightly to the outer tip. The inner and outer tips should be at the same level, and the eyebrows should never reach down at the outer tip below the outer tip of the eye. The ideal width between the brows is that of two fingers, unless the eyes are very close set. Then the width should be that of one and a half fingers. In individual cases, however, the shape of the eyebrow should follow that of the brow bone. Everyone does not have the appropriate bone formation for the arched brow.

1. BASIC BROW TYPES

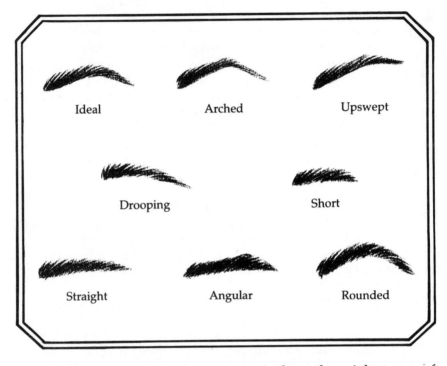

There are seven basic brow types and another eight types of distinctive eyebrows that you will encounter as you read faces. Each has its own meaning for temperament, relationships and claim to fame.

Arched Brow—Good Reputation

This is the prototype of the ideal brow—the brow of the beautiful woman and of the handsome man. It indicates one who is born to the good things in life or one who acquires them with little effort. The natural arch indicates an artistic, romantic and sensuous nature, but the smooth and tapered shape shows one also of good character who can achieve success in life and make a good name. Relationships are harmonious, and the individual is emotionally balanced, with an even temperament, and is able to use authority wisely and for the good of others as well as himself.

Upswept Brow—The Activist

This is a positive, optimistic eyebrow and is the sign of the activist, one who is aggressive, sexy, enterprising, proud, assured, ambitious and determined in the pursuit of a goal. The tail of this brow sweeps upward into the area of the forehead known as the Stagecoaches, so the individual tends to be outgoing, sweeping in his or her perspective, loving travel and inclined to be rather cavalier in human relationships. This individual enjoys exerting authority and having a wide domain for his or her activities, coupled with a desire to control. If the eyebrow is silky, smooth and well groomed, it indicates fame and good reputation through endeavors and activities outside the usual scope of events. If the eyebrow is wispy and otherwise uneven, it can indicate a dictatorial nature, with little consideration for others— a tendency to ride roughshod over intimates and employees.

Drooping Brow—The Appellant

This is the eyebrow of the naturally dependent individual; it is sometimes called the wistful brow because its owner seems to be appealing for help, looking somehow sad and forsaken. Others consider it the brow of life's natural victim. However, this eyebrow indicates one whose strength lies in apparent weakness and who can, in fact, be rather controlling and also demanding through the need for the help of others, which is often forthcoming, because people love to be needed, even imposed upon at times. This is the eyebrow affected by the early movie heroines who were often portrayed as victims or waifs (Pearl White, the early Mary Pickford), needing to be rescued by the doughty hero. The downswept tail of this eyebrow indicates one who is definitely not a doer, but one who may use sexuality as well as helplessness to achieve his or her goals. Others often regard the owner of this brow as basically weak, but the owner is usually quite strong in the sense of being self-centered and very seductive. One can be trapped totally by such an individual, and then one discovers how strong indeed is the spider's seemingly fragile web. This eyebrow can give fame through the arts, if other features support it, but often the fame is notoriety brought on by the unfortunate situations in which this person can become involved. Strength through weakness is its keynote.

Short Brow—The Challenger

This eyebrow has a youthful look, and the individual with this kind of brow is said to be an ardent lover, a passionate devotee to his or her ambitions and goals. Ambition and independence are its keynotes. The owner of this brow accepts challenges readily and often achieves success. Fame is likely to come through challenge and drive, and to be achieved at an early age. It may, however, be short-lived. The owner of this brow has a tendency to be blunt, short-tempered and somewhat fickle and uncaring in human relationships (lack of a long tip), though ardent and passionate. Relationships are often short and yet memorable. The basic desire for independence, for self-realization, can, however, take this person far, and the willingness to overcome any obstacle swiftly leads to authority. Enterprises that depend on a swift coup for success are the domain of this individual, for such a person has youthful daring that lasts through life.

Straight Brow—The Organizer

This brow shows physical strength and a level head and is the brow of the business executive. Women with this eyebrow are not content with the traditional role of homemaker but choose a career outside the home, where they prove excellent managers and meet men at their own level. The owner of this brow enjoys challenges, takes to the outdoor life and is good at sports. Nevertheless, he or she is basically an efficient organizer and manager, capable of putting affairs in order and of directing others while being clear-headed and emotionally cool. The owner of this brow, at least in business, tends to ignore the more human side of relationships (lack of outer downward tail to the eyebrow) and to think in terms of efficiency, authority and accomplishment. Often, the owner of such an eyebrow is rather cool in family relationships, too, may marry for position rather than for love and, male or female, tends to be the dominant partner and dominant parent. Neither sex, however, wants to be too involved in family life and will often turn the children over to sitters or schools, reserving the role of disciplinarian for themselves. However, both sexes also have a clear vision of their affairs and that of their business and see through pretenses. Sometimes these eyebrows make one appear scheming (if the eyebrows are heavy and allowed to grow too close together), but this is basically a youthful brow. These eyebrows may arch more with maturity, indicating that the individual's approach toward others is softening. Children with these eyebrows are very positive, self-starting and competent. The claim to fame of these eyebrows is management and clear vision.

Angular Eyebrow—The Adventurer

This wedge-shape, or knife-shape eyebrow is the sign of the adventurer. Its owner is always a dramatic personality, and fame will come through some form of showmanship or adventure. This eyebrow indicates creativity, brilliance in financial dealings and a long life to enjoy one's adventures. This individual tends to slash through obstacles, to dominate any situation and any relationship, and tends to be promiscuous rather than devoted to a single partner. You find this adventurer's eyebrow in those engaged in any form of gambling, whether it's high finance, high fashion, theater, casinos, the stock market, advertising, public relations, the military, government, merchandising, professional sports, racing and so on. This individual's life is filled with variety, adventure, plunder and narrow escapes. Weak people tend to lean on this adventurer, but the relationship is not long-lived. Our buccaneer has no time for weaklings.

Sometimes you find an individual with only one knife-shape brow; the other may be straight or normally arched. If so, the individual may have been so endowed by nature, meaning that he or she has a particularly adventurous sense of authority or command (left eyebrow knife-shape) or is intensely brilliant in the use of authority (right eyebrow knife-shape). Sometimes the individual has developed this one eyebrow crook by hours of practice before a mirror. This indicates a kind of rascality—many of the adventures this rapscallion undertakes may be legally marginal, and in human relationships, he or she is not to be trusted. Many brilliant and successful women have knife-shape brows, and they then are competing with men at their own level in finance, merchandising, fashion, show business and the like. The keynote of this brow is fame through creative brilliance and adventure.

Rounded Eyebrow—The Operator

People with this eyebrow, men or women, will be "operators" in whatever field they enter. It is the business eyebrow— and often the business is real estate, for the owner of the rounded eyebrow is highly acquisitive. The rounded brow, as you can see, exaggerates the space occupied by the Palaces of Property and also the position points of the Rainbows (Position Points 33 and 34). If this area is rounded, fatty and of good color, the person succeeds in real estate, and also in all forms of buying and selling, and usually will acquire a great many valuable possessions in life. At first glance, a woman with this eyebrow may seem self-indulgent and pampered, for she will appear very feminine. However, this conceals an extremely canny ambition and superior business acumen. Men with these eyebrows sometimes seem pompous and fussy, but they are equally well endowed with the goal of acquiring property and especially moneymaking and, again, will be most astute about business. Some entertainers, those who have made a lot of money in show business and wisely invested it, have this rounded eyebrow. Along with real estate, the stock market, merchandising and any business involved with cash flow are likely fields for these acquisitors. Usually the round-brow individual is also a clever judge of people and is very shrewd in dealing with others, combining astuteness with a seeming naivete that means they always come away with the better side of the transaction. In personal relationships, these individuals tend to dominate others—theirs is the iron hand (the Baron) in a velvet glove (the Counselor). As partners and parents, they tend to rule the family by a tight grip on the moneybags. Usually, in games of chance, they are consistent winners, because they are psychologically in charge of themselves and never become reckless and foolhardy. The important thing to note about these people is that they regard others in their lives as possessions and try to control them, manage them and profit from them. The keynote to fame with these eyebrows is possessions and business acumen.

2. SPECIAL EYEBROWS

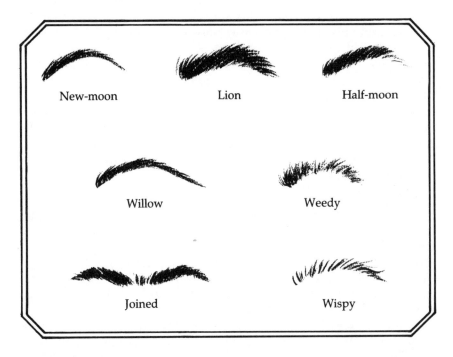

New-moon

Lion

Half-moon

Willow

Weedy

Joined

Wispy

The seven basic types of eyebrows are the ones you will most commonly encounter. But you will sometimes observe some special types, and each has a distinct meaning and denotes a particular type of person.

New-Moon Eyebrows. These crescent-shape eyebrows are very delicate and look as if they have been tweezed and shaped even if they have not. They are set very high on the forehead and usually have nice coloring and the delicate crescent form of the new moon. However, they often give the owner a kind of artificial look, as if the brows had been pasted or painted on the face. Actually, these high, delicate brows indicate a very successful and kindly person, usually one with a lot of siblings and a well-placed family. If such a person has problems, everything always seems to work out for his or her benefit. This eyebrow gives fame through high position and a kindly nature.

Lion Eyebrows. These brows are powerfully curved, thick and strong. An individual with such eyebrows looks harsh, but if the eyebrows are clean and clear, they are extremely fortunate. True, with these eyebrows, one must have large eyes. (With small eyes, there may be less benevolence.) If eyes are large, the person can achieve a very good situation—a high position and wealth. Although the actions of these individuals may be rough, deep down they are very gentle, kind and affectionate in human relationships. Once you go beyond their forbidding exterior, they are very rewarding and tender. The keynote to fame with these eyebrows is success through wealth, power and inner gentleness.

Half-Moon Eyebrows. These eyebrows take the form of a sweeping curve, with the inner part of the brow near the nose very clear and strong, while the outer tip is lighter, with loose hairs. These eyebrows, for someone with large, clear eyes, indicate a person who is friendly and can socialize well, meeting interesting and good people. An individual with longish, clear eyes finds success only after forty. The owner of these eyebrows is creative, able to manage well and achieve at his or her chosen endeavor, which will usually involve communication with people, at which this person is extremely able. Fame for the owner of these eyebrows comes through social skills and helpful, influential people.

Willow Eyebrows. These eyebrows are very thin and curved and very long, coming way down almost to the outer tip of the eye. They look as if they had been tweezed even if they haven't been. If the owner has long, slim, animated eyes, it indicates one who is very smart, alert and romantic. However, the individual is often fickle or can be too smart for his or her own good and consequently gets into trouble. Often this individual is not to be trusted in personal or business relationships, and often, alas, achieves notoriety by getting into difficulties that are gossiped about or reported in the press.

Weedy Eyebrows. These eyebrows have an irregular shape, with the hairs growing this way and that, giving an uneven, ungroomed effect. Often the eyebrows are thin and not clearly shaped. The owner of these brows is usually not clear-headed and often is suspicious. As a result, this person usually does not become too successful. If the eyebrows are also short, it is more fortunate, because the person gets into less trouble. If they are long, the owner has more troubles, and the brows indicate an unstable situation. This individual will usually not achieve fame and will probably not even make a good name; perhaps he or she will become known as someone who is suspicious and unstable.

Wispy Eyebrows. These eyebrows, whatever their basic shape, are thin, usually light in color and have long, prominent hairs standing up in them. These eyebrows usually indicate a lack of vitality and a lack of ability to exert authority over anyone, even oneself. Consequently, the individual is unable to form lasting relationships and is often sexually promiscuous, lacking control over his or her own life. The reputation of this person is consequently not very good, and there is often a lack of prudence in handling one's affairs.

Joined Brow. This is the brow of the militant and aggressive individual who has little control over temper. If the brows are otherwise well formed, the individual may succeed in professional sports, in the military or in other fields requiring aggressive attitudes. If the brows are not otherwise well formed or regular, the individual may find that her or his urge to exert authority (the Baron) is at war with common sense (the Counselor), and he or she may get in trouble with the law. It is wise for a man or woman with such eyebrows to remove the hairs that appear over the nose and thus subdue the violent stars (the eyebrows) and free the Star Point Purple Air between the eyebrows. The person thus appears less fierce and may also *feel* less fierce.

GUIDELINES

The eyebrows represent fame, a good reputation, creativity and success through intelligence and ambition and also indicate how one handles human relations. Strong, distinctive eyebrows are needed to achieve fame in public life.

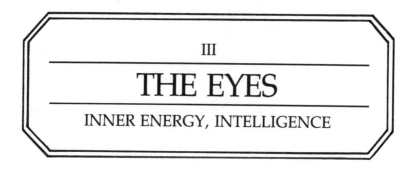

III

THE EYES

INNER ENERGY, INTELLIGENCE

The eyes represent the inner energy, which corresponds to the cosmic energies, Yin and Yang. Hence they have to do with intelligence, creativity and vitality. The eyes also are star points, and the position points for the years thirty-five to forty—the years when one can expect to shine—are in the eyes themselves. The eyes also are rivers, because they produce moisture.

The left eye represents the cosmic energy Yang, the creative, outgoing, paternal, masculine energy. It is a star point—Sun Star—and represents the father. The right eye represents cosmic energy Yin, the receptive, passive, maternal, feminine energy. The right eye is a star point—Moon Star—and represents the mother. In body organs, the eyes represent the liver.

The eyes are often considered the most revealing feature of the face. They are the organ of the sense of sight, through which we gain much of our knowledge of the world. But for the observer, they provide insight into the nature of an individual— the true nature of a person is revealed in the eyes.

When observing the eyes, consider the following features:

Size. It is considered an advantage if the eyes are large—but the size must be judged according to the size of the face and the other features. Also consider the size of the iris—the colored portion of the eye—in proportion to the eye itself. It is fortunate if the iris is large and if no white shows above or below the iris. If a lot of white shows, it indicates one who may be rash, even accident-prone. This is considered the three- or four-white-sided eye (white showing below the iris *or* above the iris as well as at the sides indicates the "three-white-sided eye"; if white shows above *and* below as well as at the sides, it is the "four-white-sided eye"), meaning the owner has a wild temper and may actually become violent.

Setting. The eyes for good fortune should not be set too close together or too far apart. Ideally, there should be the space of one eye between the two eyes. This frees the Star Point Moon Dust, which occupies this space. The eyes should be nicely full, neither protruding nor set too deep. If they are too deeply set, the individual may be reclusive. If they are protruding, the eyes lack protection (this is one of the Five Exposures and by itself is considered unfortunate).

If eyes are set too close together, it indicates overdependence on the parents, a narrow point of view and a person who tends to be weak. Disproportionately wideset eyes can show separation of the parents or a disregard of parental influence. This is often an indication of one who may possess an overpowering personality. Properly spaced eyes indicate one who is adjusted to society and in harmony with the world.

Color. The white of the eye should be very white. It is indicative of poor energy or vitality if it is yellowish, reddish or gray. However, a tinge of blue indicates a mystical, intuitive nature.

The color of the iris is also meaningful. If the iris is dark brown, it indicates vitality; blue irises show a happy nature; green irises indicate a mysterious and intellectual nature; violet eyes are indicators of a special charm and charisma. Yellow pupils warn of a display of temperament.

Brilliance. The eye should appear moist and luminous, with a controlled light or brilliance. This indicates a controlled person in whom the cosmic energies are balanced. If the eyes show a hectic glitter, as if the person were feverish, energies are overactive, and this indicates a person who is uncontrolled and perhaps dangerous. Another undesirable light is the wild or rolling eye— the mark of an individual who lacks stability and control. A kind of dullness in the eyes indicates a depletion of cosmic energy and a lack of creativity and perhaps intelligence.

If the eyes are luminous and bright or sparkling, it reveals energies and intelligence under control and creativity directed into positive channels.

Lashes. Long lashes show one who is soft-hearted, sensitive and spiritual. Short lashes indicate one who is strong and aggressive. If lashes are thin and loose or sparse, it denotes inactivity, sluggishness, poor circulation.

Eyelids. The eyelids should be reasonably thick to give protection and covering to the eye. This is considered fortunate in that it assures normal sensuality and will. If the eyelids are very thick, it indicates a deeply sensuous nature and strong-mindedness. If they are very thin, the individual may lack the capacity for sensuous pleasure and also be a guarded, insecure individual.

Eye Lines. One crease in the upper lid is normal and gives the eye dimension. If this crease is missing, the individual may be materialistic but have good insight. If there is more than one horizontal line on the upper lid and also on the lower lid, it indicates watchfulness, perhaps a suspicious nature. Crow's feet at the outer corners of the eye indicate promiscuity.

The Ideal Eye. The ideal eye—that is, ideal for what the eye represents (intelligence, creativity and inner energy)—is large, full and well set, with the space of one eye between the eyes. The white is very white and clear but does not dominate the eye or show above or below the iris. The light of the eye is luminous and controlled, and the lids are medium thick, with full, strong lashes; the skin around the eyes is unlined. The person with such an eye, say the Chinese, is intelligent, courageous, artistic, sensitive and capable of leadership. This eye shows a balance of the inner energies.

1. BASIC EYE TYPES

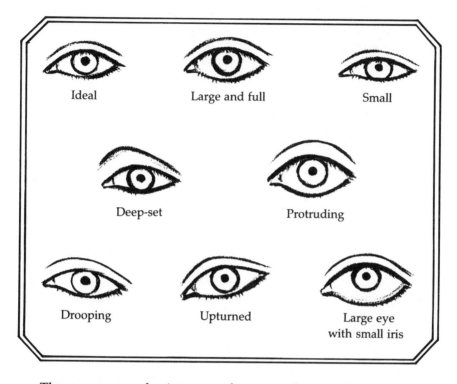

| Ideal | Large and full | Small |

| Deep-set | Protruding |

| Drooping | Upturned | Large eye with small iris |

There are seven basic types of eyes, and most of the eyes you observe will fall into one or another of these categories. However, there are also six other special types of eyes, which you will encounter only occasionally but which you will want to understand, because these are often the sign of very fascinating people. When you are evaluating the eye type, also consider the placement on the face, the setting, the color and other points already suggested.

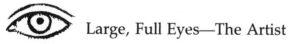 Large, Full Eyes—The Artist

This eye is close to the ideal eye but fuller, showing one who is naturally outgoing—intelligent, sensitive and artistic. This person is open and frank and makes a fine leader. The large-eyed individual also succeeds in the theater and other arts, for he or she is an excellent observer. Women with these eyes, however, do not make good homemakers, because they want to be out in the world, sharing a broader experience. It is sometimes a roving eye, because the natural eroticism of this eye quickly attracts sexual partners, and those with this eye are usually attention-getters. The vitality—inner energy—of the owner of these eyes is high, and the ability to direct this energy intelligently is a quality of the one with large, full eyes. Here is a person who often becomes a star, who is always popular among people and one who is admired and frequently esteemed. The years thirty-four to forty are usually outstanding for this person, because he or she tends to live a full life during this Star Period.

Small Eyes—The Introspective

This eye is small in comparison with the rest of the face. Be sure you are really looking at small eyes and not merely at deep-set eyes. Small eyes show one who is loyal in relationships but often self-satisfied about accomplishments and perhaps given too much to introspection. People often find this person hard to get to know, somewhat unapproachable; and the individual is not easily won over. He or she often has somewhat narrow standards and tends to judge others too harshly. When involved in a relationship, this person can be very devoted and steadfast, loyal and committed—but alas, he or she also tends to be jealous and can fail to express it, letting the jealousy seethe inside, which often leads to lack of communication between partners. Don't think, however, that small eyes indicate someone who is mean and petty. On the contrary, these people can be very intense and giving when they are moved to be so. They tend, though, to be self-complacent and satisfied with their abilities and do not try to extend themselves into large areas of achievement. Many people in the graphic arts, researchers, students who become experts in a field, craftspeople, poets and writers have small eyes. The problem here is that the person can take a diminished view of life and see things only in a narrow focus, not exerting the command that his or her native intelligence merits. These people tend to be perfectionists, and the period of the late thirties when their position points fall in the eye area is often the time when they get their lives together exactly as they want them to be. That they do not expand their horizons to take in a vaster canvas should not be held against them. However, recognize that they are likely to be smug about their work, no matter how limited it seems to others, and need praise, not a push.

 ## Deep-Set Eyes—The Dreamer

As their deep-set eyes suggest, these people tend to be *deep.* They are romantic dreamers, intellectual and often inspired, but they are also extremely good at money matters. As a result, they are rewarding partners and are able to provide for their own financial needs, often by developing systems—for playing the horses or the stock market—or even by being very canny at trades and at buying and selling. This talent is often unsuspected by others, who see them as philosophers and poets. True, these people like to go into the thinking areas of life—the professions. Many become writers, researchers, sometimes inventors. They are rarely impulsive and tend to be conservative in their approach to most matters of the world, more intellectual than physical. Others need to respect their innate sensitivity and romanticism, because they are easily hurt if their dreams are violated or if reality is imposed upon their fantasies. Because they are inward people, they often do not fully realize the stardom that others achieve in their late thirties, when the position points fall in the eyes. However, this is sometimes a turning point for these people, and often after age thirty-five, they become more realistic and also more outgoing. These people make good advisers, because they can think quite clearly about another's problems—more so, perhaps, than about their own—and will often put a new, unexpected light over a matter that a more worldly person has not considered. The problem of deep-set eyes is that, unless more outgoing features rescue them, the owners can become lost in fantasy in their young and middle years and become too unrealistic to cope totally with the world around them.

Protruding Eyes—The Gambler

This eye marks one who takes chances and is always looking for an opportunity to venture in a new direction. The fullness shows one who is outgoing, strong-minded, often willful and perhaps also improvident. But this is not always true. The person with this eye sees what is going on and knows when to draw back as well as to gamble, and because of this strong insight, he or she is often a winner. This individual is an extrovert and can be rash and impulsive but can also be warm and helpful, tending to recognize quickly the needs of others. It is easy for this person to make complete changes in life-style, location and work, for the tendency is always to take a chance. They are easily tempted by a new opportunity.

This is a person who can be strong and exert control over others, and who prefers a dominant position. But it is also one who tends to be sexually indulgent and who takes risks in relationships as well as in money and work. These people succeed in areas where risks are high, both physical and monetary, and often reach the late thirties with a fairly good position assured. However, this is a time when they tend to risk everything again and will have utmost confidence in their ability to recoup any losses. This individual does not need to play it safe, either, in relationships or business enterprises—and if other features show the person to be lucky, this is a good eye to follow.

Basically the nature is earthy, not at all introspective, and the person feels little responsibility and few qualms if there is no money left from a gamble to pay the rent. Usually, they snap back. This individual is strong-minded and can get control over others and talk others into their way of doing things. Money can easily walk out of your pocket into theirs.

These individuals succeed where it is necessary to command the attention of others, to get matters off to a fast start, to introduce a kind of charisma into everyday enterprises. They are always ready to make a deal and a fast buck. Nongamblers find it hard to understand the reckless life of this type of person, but the person with these eyes suffers none of the qualms you might feel about living such a chancy life. They are always able to spot a way out of a tight corner.

Upturned Eyes—The Optimist

When you meet someone with these eyes, you know you are encountering a cheerful person with a sharp sense of humor, who is quick-witted, alert and mischievous. You may not know this is also a short-tempered person who can snap quickly into a jealous rage and react with a tantrum when frustrated. But such shortcomings often accompany these tip-tilted eyes. Good qualities abound—the person is optimistic, brave, a bit of an adventurer, one who may be opportunistic but who is also confident and decisive. This is an idea person, someone who catches on quickly to the nut of a situation and acts. Here you find enthusiasm and excitement along with wit, quick intelligence and conviviality; an easy conversationalist.

This person thrives best on work that offers quickly achieved short-term goals, where things happen fast, where he or she can be on the move, meet people, make superficial contacts; in short, where there is action and where the individual can flaunt her or his flair. These eyes are kindest to the young—those under forty—and probably the career is well set up by the time they reach the thirties. The years from thirty-five to forty are starring ones for this jaunty optimist, who can quickly take advantage of any situation that is offered.

In relationships, this person often shows a negative side. So long as it is a fun situation, our optimist is chatty, lively and considerate. But in clinches, the short temper, the unreasonable demands and the quick jealousy may show the person to be completely unreliable, and a relationship can be fragmented before it fully sets. There is a tendency to be wantonly disruptive of stability, and this can drive a security-minded partner out of his or her mind. This is not to say that some of these people do not become aware of their problems and get their impishness under control; they often do in later years. Others merely become cantankerous. This person will always be stimulating in the short run, but it may be wise to let him or her love you and leave you.

Drooping Eyes—The Easy Mark

This has been called the weeping eye because its owner somehow looks sad and seems to smile through her or his tears. The outer corners of the eyes are lower than the inner corners, and this creates a wistful look. If this person also has drooping eyebrows (they do not always go together), the effect is exaggerated.

This eye shows one who is likely to be considerate of others to a fault, self-effacing, submissive, even masochistic, very eager to be helpful but silently asking to be helped, *please*. This person often gets involved in a kind of seesaw relationship, trying to help someone, who then drags the helper down into a morass from which he or she finds it difficult to become extricated, finally needing help to be restored. There is a kind of flow between submissiveness and a desire to control that somehow manages to be ineffectual. However, this person is basically good, and often is found in the helping professions, truly trying to express compassion for those whose need is greater or more immediate than his or her own.

The asset of this individual is a true appreciation of the problems of others, and although the person does not want to have much responsibility, he or she is able to give sympathy and understanding, possessing as a prime asset a kind of emotional intelligence that is much needed in the world.

In personal relationships, this person may be slipshod, often pairing with the wrong person. Others with this eye find what they truly need—a strong partner who likes someone dependent and who provides a bulwark against the world. When this happens, the droopy-eyed person often develops a kind of assurance, pride and devotion that leads to a useful life showing consideration for others. When several faulty relationships have already been experienced by age thirty-five, the late thirties often become the time when a lasting partnership can be established.

 ## Large Eye with Small Iris—The Rebel

This is called the three-white-sided eye, because the white of the eye shows below the iris (and sometimes above, making it a four-white-sided eye) as well as at the sides. With a small iris, there is a lot of white showing, and this gives the individual a hunted look, as if he or she is always on the lookout for an attacker. This is the eye of the rebel, the troublemaker, the restless, the unreliable, even the unscrupulous. The individual with a small iris is shrewd, and the person with an excess of white is adventurous, but between these two qualities, the individual can become basically restless, always wanting more than he or she has, always seeking to take advantage of others, to use them and to evade responsibility. The inner energy is erratic, and the orientation is toward change and short-term relationships. So, this person tends to change jobs, field of enterprise and especially partners often. Basically, this individual can be generous, but this shows itself in a tendency to lose money and possessions, a kind of carelessness about reputation and attitudes. The white of the eye also seems to attract unwholesome people, so that this individual is also the victim of bad company as well as of his or her own restless nature. The years from thirty-five to forty, when the position points fall in the eye, are often a time of crisis, when opportunities are squandered due to a lack of ability to follow through on advantages and a need to disrupt relationships. A kind of discontent often overwhelms the person at this period, when life can be frittered away in a series of fresh starts.

2. SPECIAL EYES

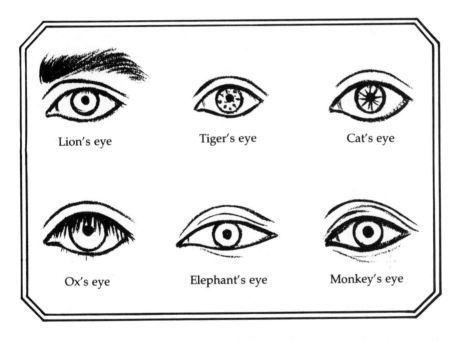

Lion's eye

Tiger's eye

Cat's eye

Ox's eye

Elephant's eye

Monkey's eye

These special eyes are named for various animal types and always denote a very special kind of person, usually with a distinctive and notable intellect.

Lion's Eyes. These are large eyes, usually with thick eyebrows, which are notable for their strong focus. They may, in fact, be almost overpowering when you encounter them.

And their owner is indeed a powerful person. However, these eyes denote a very honest and straightforward nature—one who is charitable and very giving to others. This individual is always successful and has a very long life.

Tiger's Eyes. These eyes are very round and short, and the irises have gold flecks. Again, they denote a wealthy and powerful person with a very strong character—one who will become wealthy, however, only after age forty. This person is often very stern with family and may become alienated from them because he or she is *too* strong and becomes bossy and domineering.

Cat's Eyes. Again, the eyes are very round, but they show an interesting glitter and have a kind of yellowish cast. This person is very magnetic and influences others. The cat-eyed person is colorful and competitive, longs to be surrounded by beauty and loves to spend money, and so is very self-indulgent.

Ox Eyes. Again, these eyes are very large and round, with large pupils and very long, thick, straight lashes. These eyes belong to very good, patient and pleasant people who enjoy a long life and are very nice to be around.

Elephant's Eyes. The eyes are not large but they tend to be long, with a shape like a double lid above and below, so that they appear to have wavy lines around the eyes. These people enjoy pleasure and a peaceful existence, are reasonably successful and well off and can look forward to a very long life.

Monkey Eyes. The eyes are very deep and dark and show a lot of lid, with two or three lines above and below. The eyes move around a lot, as if the individual is always on the alert. These people tend to look and learn. They may be too conservative and are likely to be worriers. But financially and otherwise, they usually turn out all right. The woman with these eyes may be successful, but she seems never to calm down and may be almost neurotic about keeping busy.

GUIDELINES

Evaluate the eyes according to their size, shape, setting on the face, color, the amount of white showing, the lids and lines and the length of the lashes as well as their specific type. Eyes represent inner energy, so whatever the character of the eye, it is their luminosity or glow that is particularly significant.

IV

THE NOSE

WEALTH, ACHIEVEMENT IN MID-LIFE

The nose is a mountain, and is often the most prominent feature of the face. In face reading, it represents wealth and achievement in career—the ability to find opportunity, to accumulate or waste wealth. A prominent nose is considered an asset to wealth and success.

The nose begins at Position Point 41, called the Root of the Mountain, which is located at the root of the nose in the Star Point Moon Dust between the eyes. This is also an important middle point. On the bridge—the bony part of the nose—lie two other significant middle points, Point 44 (Sitting on Top of One's Age) and Point 45 (Sitting on Top of One's Longevity). Point 48—the Peak of Perfection, the Throne of the Emperor—is on the tip of the nose in the Palace of Wealth. So the nose actually represents the long climb to success and wealth that most people experience in the decade of the forties.

When you are observing the nose, consider it in terms of its value for success in career and wealth as well as in terms of its meaning to one's human relationships of marriage and family life.

Points 49 and 50 are on the nostrils, and the flare of the nostrils is also significant, showing how the person handles money, work and human relations.

The nose is also a planet point—it represents the planet Saturn, Earth Star, and so has much to do with the stabilization that takes place in mid-life, the years of the Second Station. The planet Saturn also gives its color to the nose, which should be peachy pink.

Among body organs, the nose represents the lungs and the male sex organ.

EVALUATING THE NOSE

Begin your evaluation of the nose by considering its size, its prominence—its stature as a mountain—its support and its color.

Prominence. It is considered favorable if the nose is large—prominent and outstanding.

Support. Observe whether the nose is alone on a plain—the single outstanding feature—or whether it is supported by other mountains—a prominent forehead, cheekbones and chin. It is considered favorable if the nose is the most prominent mountain but is supported by other prominent features. If the nose is alone on the plain, it loses value whatever its positive characteristics may be. However, it should have space. Other mountains, such as the cheekbones, should not be too close to it.

Color. Observe the color—the nose should be beigy pink—not too red and not too pale and not discolored or greenish. If the nose is too red, it is a signal that its owner may be extravagant and a wastrel, and that the temper may be short. If the nose is too pale, particularly if the bridge of the nose is whitish, it shows a lack of vitality and perhaps illness, a lack of the stamina needed to carry oneself to the peak.

Grayish color on the nose indicates ailments; greenish, a default and perhaps a confinement. Purplish color, however, indicates a promotion. The fortunate pinky beige tone promises good fortune in money matters.

The nose should also have shine. This promises prosperity and high honors and a rise in position. A dullish look to the nose negates these benefits.

Next observe the three major parts of the nose, starting at the root.

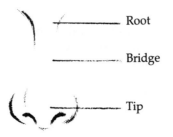

The Root. The root of the nose starts at Position Point 41, the Star Point Moon Dust, in the Palace of Health. The root of the nose should be clear and smooth, with good color to give the vitality needed for the climb to success. If it is rough or lumpy, it can indicate a poor start and also domestic problems. If the root is hollow, it can have poor indications for health and long life as well as for success in business and family life.

If it is flat and broad, it shows the ability to create a warm, satisfying family life and a comfortable family business. If it is high, the root promises strength in enterprises involving work and family and also a long life in which to enjoy success.

The Bridge. The middle, bony part of the nose, the bridge, should be straight for good health and vitality and a chance to live long in order to develop one's capacities. Points 44 and 45 on the bridge of the nose are both health points, so this area indicates the vitality and good health needed to assure success in life.

If it is thin and bony, it can indicate one who is hypercritical and too self-centered to do well at work or in family life. A bony hump at the bridge increases this hyperactive tendency.

If the nose is flat in this area, you have to work hard all your life to make a living.

The Tip. The tip of the nose should be well rounded to assure you of wealth and success—this rounded tip is one of the best features to have if you are interested in money. If the tip is thin and sharp, money does not come easy. If you inherit it, you will be very stingy.

The Nostrils. The flare of the nostrils indicates how you handle money. Ideally, the nostril wings are rounded and slightly flared, showing wise use of money and normal charity. If the nostrils are full and flared, you are likely to be outgoing and generous. If the nostrils are thin and pinched, you may be miserly and money-grubbing.

If the nostril flare is well proportioned and in balance with the size of the nose, it is helpful to any success and wealth the nose promises. If the nostril flares are large in proportion to the nose, they indicate a tendency to lose money. If they are wide and flaring, you can become a self-made millionaire. Small, narrow nostril flares in proportion to the size of the nose suggest caution in money-making. If the nostrils are very thin and flat, the owner has trouble making money or holding onto it.

The nostrils, of course, are rivers, and they should appear moist and they should not be exposed. Exposed nostril openings show a lack of modesty and tact. In addition, this is one of the Five Exposures, any one of which singly is unlucky.

The Ideal Nose. The ideal nose—ideal, that is, for the qualities the nose represents (wealth, success in the middle years, good family life and achievement)—is prominent, stands out from the face and is not too crowded by other mountains. The whole line of the nose is well-formed from base to tip.

It is smooth and well formed at the root for a good start in career and a stable family life. The bridge is straight and well formed for health and vitality in the middle years and a chance to live long enough to develop one's capacities. The tip is well rounded, and the nostril wings are rounded and slightly flared.

With this nose, one can expect achievement in life, honors, health, wealth, good family and friends.

1. BASIC NOSE SHAPES

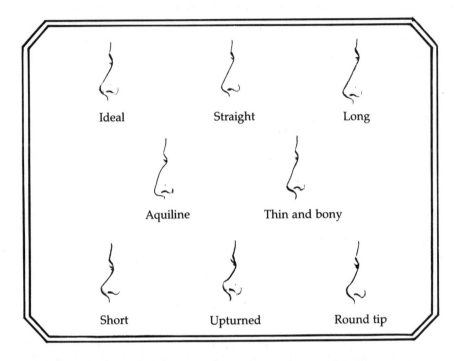

There are seven basic nose shapes, and most of the noses you observe will fall into one or another of these categories. There are also six animal-type noses that occur less frequently, but when they do, they indicate an unusual person.

Straight—The Ethical Nose

This is a successful nose and financially a good nose—you can read from it at once that the person behind it will be straight in any dealings—honest, even-tempered, enterprising and likely to reach a high position in life. The person usually enjoys good health and vitality and a stable family life. This is the nose of someone you can admire and trust, who will treat others equally in any situation and be tolerant of the shortcomings of others.

The person with this nose often seems to have achieved success easily. Without seemingly great effort, things fall into his or her lap. What is more likely to be true is that the owner of this nose is competent, effective and doesn't make waves or put obstacles in his or her own way. This person chooses and follows a direction to a goal and steadily builds achievement upon achievement, winning the support of family, co-workers and friends by good nature and kindly tolerance. Vitality and health are also supportive to a long, successful life.

Long—The Rational Nose

This is the nose of a conservative and rational individual, someone who is likely to choose one of the professions demanding a logical mind, clear thinking and a conservative viewpoint. Often, however, this individual is somewhat uncompromising, both because he or she is overdemanding and intolerant of the weaknesses and shortcomings of others. The individual often expects others to be as sane and controlled as himself and will be unprepared for the things that always go wrong because of human error. With this nose, one can act intelligently and control one's own feelings, but assets must usually be built gradually, and much long-range planning is needed to guarantee stability and wealth in old age. This individual may also be artistic and creative, but then usually in a more traditional field of the arts, and he or she is by no means avant-garde. Security is important to this individual, and the necessary adjustments of the middle years may be difficult to make because of the stand-pat, rather unyielding nature. With this nose, however, one has time to construct a good life, as creative and intellectual abilities develop early and are put on a constructive course. This person should not be persuaded to take sudden chances or to gamble all on a get-rich-quick scheme in the middle years. It's the planning and thinking through before action that gets him or her to the goal.

Aquiline—The Acquisitive Nose

The high bridge and long tip of this nose, if it is well fleshed, give a tremendous capacity for achievement and wealth and also for sexual vitality. This is a nose for money, a nose for power and a nose for a fascinating and interesting life in pursuing success.

People with this nose go into business for pleasure, because they enjoy the capacity to make a smart deal, to accumulate wealth, to outdo others and to compete strongly in the marketplace. Businessmen and women, industrialists, financial wizards, merchants and manufacturers with this nose succeed. Those with this nose also often have a good sense of smell and seem to have a talent for sniffing out a good deal and also for catching the odor of anything that isn't right when they deal with less than honorable people. The enjoyment of competition, of acquiring the good things in life and displaying wealth are characteristic of this nose. It is also the mark of entrepreneurs, military conquerors and many politicians. Usually you will find this nose on one who has achieved many of the good things of life and has the capacity to enjoy them.

Thin and Bony—The Perfectionist Nose

This nose is often considered the mark of the beautiful woman and the handsome male and has about it an arrogance and pride that once belonged to the patricians. Often, its owner is self-centered, hypercritical, a perfectionist with a desire to command and control but with little human tolerance of others. The thin, bony bridge is considered negative for happy family life—the individual is too critical and self-centered to make others want to be involved—and if the tip is also pointed, it can indicate one who lacks pleasure in material things as well. Among those born to status and wealth, the nose is all right, because this person can often indulge in a solitary, demanding life. But if these assets are missing, the person will often become a little mean about money, even miserly, and will not be able to achieve a great deal or accumulate much wealth. This can result in an unhappy, dissatisfied person unless other features on the face denote compensations.

Short—The Enthusiastic Nose

This nose shows an enthusiastic, optimistic person who enjoys life and is sociable, friendly, open-minded and outgoing but probably has only short-term goals and is often not very ambitious, worrying little about the future. If the nose is well fleshed, the individual gets along all right financially, but otherwise, the short nose shows a lack of the time and calculation needed to make a fortune. Money, if it comes, arrives in short spurts and does not have staying power. This individual, being enthusiastic, is a willing helper and a fun person to be around; he or she makes friends easily and cheers on others. Don't expect a powerful career out of this optimistic character, who doesn't even think about such things. This tends to be a young nose—someone who does well in the earlier years but seems to lose out a little in mid-life, when everyone else is achieving. However, this nose always attracts opportunity, even if the strength to make good on chances is not present. This person may have a short interest span—even in personal relationships—and will make changes often and seemingly for no reason. These people often do not get deeply involved in family life, but they are honest, good-hearted and cheerful, and they take acquaintances and life situations as they are, without complaining, making the best of what is available and cheerfully accepting the short end of the stick, if that is what life offers them.

Upturned—The Spendthrift Nose

This nose usually indicates someone who is cheerful, unconventional, a free spender—a lighthearted individual who doesn't worry about the future and often wastes today. Generous and considerate, the owner of this nose bounces back readily from any setback and happily starts out again on a new enterprise. This person is optimistic and usually finds friends and helpers easily—everyone wants to give him or her a fresh chance. Because he or she is fun to be around, this person finds it easy to get a job, but also to lose one. The Peak of Perfection—the tip of this nose—is very high, so the individual feels successful even when he or she is not. This may lead to fantasies of achievement when no effort has yet been made. It is a head-in-the-air psychology. Very generous with money, this person also is generous sexually and, alas, cannot keep a secret.

This is again a young nose, and the person who possesses it starts out well, but in the middle years success may be elusive, and the chance to get fresh starts diminishes as the person reaches the forties. This upturned nose also exposes the nostril openings (one of the Five Exposures), which, by nature, is unfortunate if it is the only exposure. With the other four, however, this nose indicates a superfortunate person. If the tip of this nose is well fleshed, even fat, the individual may be able to make quick, easy money, although he or she usually will get rid of it just as speedily.

Round Tip—The Accumulative Nose

A nice round tip on the nose is the best asset for accumulating money. It's very wise to associate yourself with such a nose when you are entering any business deal or partnership and also when you are marrying, because you will then be well provided for. One of the secrets of the wealth of this round-tip nose is that it also denotes a warm, gentle-hearted, kind and self-sacrificing individual, one who has qualities that endear, and win support, loyalty and friendship. Here is a case of bread thrown upon the waters returning a hundredfold, because you will find in this individual one who also is willing to help out a friend or family member in an emergency and never mention the matter. This is not, however, usually a get-rich-quick, entrepreneurial fast-buck nose. Instead, it accumulates wealth through work, providence, good care of possessions and association with worthy people—all stable Saturn (Earth Star) qualities. Material things are usually accumulated, too, and this person lives well and comfortably, achieving stability in career and family life in the forties, when the characteristics of the nose are most effective. The individual always ends up financially well off and able to enjoy the things that money can buy.

2. SPECIAL NOSES

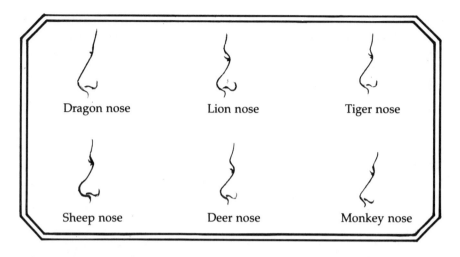

Dragon nose   Lion nose   Tiger nose

Sheep nose   Deer nose   Monkey nose

There are six special noses—animal-type noses—of which five are very lucky and just one is less so.

Dragon Nose. This is the best kind of nose to have. Its owner gets everything and has enough to pass on to others, can achieve power and wealth and become great. This nose has a good root—it's not too thin and comes down straight from the forehead without an indentation. The peak is straight and rounded; the nostrils are straight and close to the nose, with a nice glow, and they're slightly rounded, too. When you encounter this nose, you are up against an extremely important person.

Lion's Nose. Its owner will be industrious and can build a business empire and accumulate wealth and possessions. This nose is very big, flat at the bridge and the tip is basically rounded, with rounded unexposed nostrils, very generous in size.

Tiger Nose. Its owner will be famous and can build a nice name and have a fine home and family. This nose has a straight bridge but is basically rounded, with rounded nostrils, but the nostril openings are not exposed and the nostrils are slightly flat, very straight at the sides and rounded at the top.

Sheep Nose. The owner of this nose can become extremely wealthy. This nose is unusually large, with a Peak of Perfection that is very big and rounded. The nostrils are large, but the openings don't show.

Deer Nose. This person is very kind and also very fortunate. He or she gets out of trouble easily, has a long life and will be successful in later years. This nose is slightly flat at the root and straight; there is little bone in the bridge, and the nose is somewhat flat here. The root is narrow and the peak is rounded, not long or bony.

Monkey Nose. This nose is small but not flat, set very close to the upper lip, and has nostrils that are very flat. The peak is reddish in color. This nose does not accumulate much money; the nature is suspicious, and its owner will find it hard to achieve great success.

GUIDELINES

The nose should be prominent and rounded at the tip for wealth and success.

First, evaluate the basic shape of the nose; then mentally modify it according to the flare of the nostrils, the color and other characteristics that give it greater value or detract from its promise.

Remember that the qualities of the nose are most effective in the years of the forties.

Will a nose correction change the fortune? When you observe a nose, it may not be the one nature provided but one which has been shaped by a cosmetic surgeon. With experience, you will be able to recognize a nose job and also perhaps discern the shape of the original nose from the other facial contours. Many people who have had their nose reshaped say it has changed their lives—they have become happier, more adjusted and more acceptable. However, the question of whether they are richer or poorer as a consequence cannot be completely settled. We are inclined to think that to exchange a nice fat comfortable nose for a haughty one might not be a worthwhile trade financially.

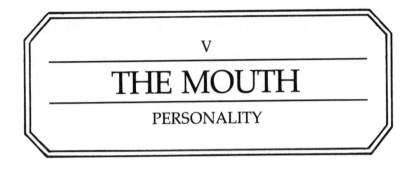

V

THE MOUTH

PERSONALITY

The mouth represents the personality. As a feature, the mouth partakes of the cosmic energy Yin—emotional, perceptive, feminine—and reveals the human emotive nature, the sensuality and expressiveness of an individual. The mouth is the key to expression in the face, and if it can be said that the eyes do not lie, then it is equally true that the mouth can betray—it reveals the emotional vulnerability, the "heart."

Just as the nose represents the male sex organ, the mouth represents the female sex organ; however, among the body organs, the lips represent the spleen.

The mouth is the feature related to the planet Mercury, Water Star; its color is best when it is rosy red. And because the mouth is a river, it should appear moist. A too-pale or too-dry mouth indicates a lack of emotional energy—a paling or drying up of the personality, even a lack of communication and understanding.

The mouth is among the most eloquent features. Many traits can be discovered by observing the mouth.

- If the lips are thin or kept tightly drawn, the person is naturally stubborn. Do not push this person too far.
- If the mouth is always kept slightly open, it indicates sexual indulgence.
- A thin upper lip with a full lower lip shows one who is highly competitive, who excels and who enjoys a good argument.
- A good, firm, mobile mouth indicates a person of integrity, good health and pleasing personality.
- A short upper lip that exposes the teeth creates one of the Five Exposures—if it is not accompanied by the other four, it indicates difficulties, perhaps a lack of discipline or poverty.

The mouth is the major feature of the Third Station (maturity) of the face—its position point is 60. The significance here is that by the time we reach this part of life, we are truly dependent for happiness on our personality and our relationships with others— and by this time, the personality should be fully mature. The mouth is, however, a feature that often changes much with the years. Keeping the mouth firm, mobile and expressive into maturity is a sign of continuing vitality and enjoyment of life.

The mouth is associated with the sense of taste, food, speech, expressiveness, smiling, kissing and other pleasures—all indicators of its Yin (emotional) nature. Much can be learned about a person from the basic shape of the mouth, but consider as well the color, the moistness of the lips and the general contour and mobility of the mouth, as well as its firmness and texture.

The Ideal Mouth. Ideally—that is, ideal for the personality qualities indicated by the mouth—the lips should be fairly full, firm and well shaped, with a definite contour. They should be full and rounded, with the upper and lower lip of equal fullness and the indentation in the upper lip well defined. The corners of upper and lower lips should meet exactly and be clear-cut. The contour of the lower lip is ideally slightly squared to give firmness and definite shape.

1. BASIC MOUTH SHAPES

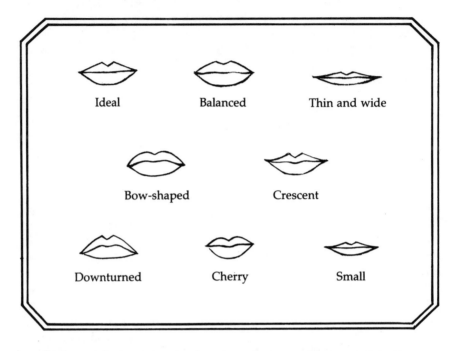

There are seven basic mouth shapes, and most mouths you see will fall into one or another of these categories. There also are four special mouths that relate to the animal types, and the owners of these mouths are indeed exceptional people.

Balanced Mouth—The Integrated Personality

In this mouth, the lips are of equal fullness, and the corners meet exactly so that there is a kind of balance immediately apparent. People with such mouths are balanced and friendly, revealing warmth, charm and good fellowship. They usually are responsible members of society and manage to achieve a good position in life. They are even tempered, warmhearted and charming. These people are basically adaptable—they smile easily and enjoy spontaneous laughter. Their nature is expressive, and usually these individuals have good health and vitality and a responsive sexuality. They handle people well and find it easy to deal with the public, to solve problems and to adjust to changes with a minimum of fuss. The men are genial hosts, the women gracious hostesses, and they usually bring up their children well. Because of their basic equanimity, they are great to have around in a crisis and can often take command in a difficult situation. If you need to rely on this person, he or she will not fail you. They seem to balance an interest in all aspects of life—work, art, family, and play—and do not create problems for themselves or for others.

Thin, Wide Mouth—The Commander

Here is someone who likes to take command, exert authority, in fact, boss others around—friends, family and fellow workers. The owner of this mouth tends to be rigid; he or she is strong-minded, proud and firm in decisions. Luckily, this person can often be generous, good-hearted and smooth tempered. But the need to run things his or her way can lead to hostility from others that often causes them to overlook the better qualities. Children of a parent with such a mouth are usually well brought up and firmly disciplined and are often the better for it. In a showdown, these people stand by you and will always back you up. However, they often also stand by their own decisions, right or wrong, and do not easily back down from any postion they take. People with this mouth do well in positions of authority, but they can also work for others, because they accept self-discipline as well. If this mouth is firm as well as thin and wide, the more rigid qualities will be dominant. If the mouth is mobile and the person smiles easily, the more generous and compatible qualities emerge. However, this is always someone who tries to dominate others and the situation in order to take the lead. The personality behind this mouth is often not very sensual. Sometimes these people may become more easygoing with age, although you should not count on it. They tend to be talkers, not listeners, and so often are not aware of what others think and feel.

Bow-Shape Mouth—The Cynic

This mouth has lips that are full and rounded, but the corners meet on a level that is often that of the curve of the lower lip, so the mouth looks pouty, petulant and dissatisfied, which this person often is. He or she is frequently self-centered and impersonal as well. Although the mouth appears sensual, the person may merely be self-indulgent and seek pleasure in food rather than in people. Oddly, this individual likes the company of others but not their companionship—he or she will be aloof in a crowd and not easy to get to know. People with this type of mouth often appear to be interesting; we feel there must be a knowing personality behind this somewhat cruel and indifferent mouth. But it is not easy to find, and often the person will prove as superficial as the attitude he or she displays.

This is not to say that such a mouth is all-alienating. These people do well in any sphere of life where they can play a part. And they often play the role given them supremely well, because they are fantasists at heart. Once this person has been able to give his or her confidence to another and feels really loved and accepted, the defenses break down and the person can indeed become loving if not giving. Unfortunately, their very cynicism often brings on negative relationships. Because this mouth tends to widen in later years, the person can often broaden his or her viewpoint in maturity, and as relationships tend to become less poignantly personal as one matures, some building blocks of a relationship can be laid.

Crescent Mouth—The Humorist

This mouth turns up at the corners and has a cheerful look. If the indentation in the upper lip is also deep, it shows someone who is cheerful and optimistic, has a great sense of humor and is fun to be around. Such a person is active, creative and well liked by others. Crescent-mouthed individuals laugh a lot, smiling even at misfortune, but they are highly sensitive, too. They like to be with people and succeed wherever they have to meet the public and make others comfortable and at ease with themselves. As writers, cartoonists, artists and comedians, they star, and whatever they do, they add a light touch that promotes a sense of well-being and enthusiasm. People with such a mouth seem never to be bored; they do tend to flit from one thing to another, being basically somewhat restless, but they are not really irresponsible. As parents, these people have fun and enjoy their offspring, creating a pleasing ambiance. There is something always youthful and attractive about them; even in their later years, they look younger and act and feel younger than they are. The wonderful thing about this mouth is its built-in smile that seems always to be cheering others on, finding something to be glad about. Don't expect this humorist to take you too seriously, however, and if you can't laugh your troubles away, go elsewhere for help in a crisis. There is some tendency to be just a bit superficial, a little unconcerned about the future or even present predicaments. Sometimes these cheerful optimists get bogged down in humdrum work just because they think mostly of getting along and not digging in. Women with this mouth tend to be butterflies; men often take their responsibilities somewhat more seriously, perhaps because life demands it. However, men, too, tend to be the life of the party and always add an upbeat note to any get-together.

Downturned Mouth—The Demander

In this mouth, the corners tend to droop, and often the owner of this mouth tends to keep it slightly open. So, the effect is one of mouth-breathing and also, unfortunately, of discontent. More women than men seem to have this mouth, but in either sex, it shows one who is a taker, not a giver, one who tends to be greedy in his or her demands—whether for love, money, sex or recognition—and is never quite satisfied with what life bestows. In spite of the effect of gullibility that this mouth gives, the owner is likely to be highly demanding, strong-willed, domineering and not easily influenced by others. And in spite of their demands upon others, the owners of such a mouth are themselves rather lazy and self-indulgent—they tend to resent being given responsibility, although they like to order others about.

This mouth also shows a deeply sensual nature and often indicates one who is loose or careless in sexual indulgences without attempting to get into a responsive relationship. There is often a lack of humor, a tendency to be depressed or to be overserious about their own problems and needs as a way of justifying their own refusal not to take responsibility for themselves and to expect others to supply their needs on demand. They tend to press people out of their lives and then feel neglected, which does not lead to the satisfaction they seek and crave. With this mouth, look to other features in the face that can compensate for its somewhat negative implications.

Cherry Mouth—The Comforter

This full, round mouth is shaped like a kiss and carries with it the implication of a gentle, quiet, kind and loving nature. A woman with this mouth is said to be the perfect wife—loving, docile, obedient, tender, warm and quiet in nature. Males with this mouth are not necessarily effeminate, but they are men who have highly developed the Yin side of their nature—the emotional, cultural energy—and have in abundance the qualities of sympathy, affection, and understanding, often along with an appreciation of the cultural side of life. You find them frequently as curators of antiquities or the arts, as reviewers and historians, appreciators of the arts rather than creators. These men also often have an uncommon appreciation of women and can offer a kind of empathy and friendship that is not usually found in one of the opposite sex. Women with this mouth tend to marry young and well and to mature as parent, hostess, and appreciator, too. They are imaginative, poetical as well as practical; and they create a very cozy environment for spouse and children. The men tend to stay bachelors or marry late in life, because they enjoy creating their own home and environment, are often a bit of the bon vivant, and although they like a wide circle of interesting people, they prefer to live alone. In either sex, this mouth represents a loving and tender personality, one who will be very interesting to those who can enter into their comfortable circle.

Small Mouth—The Loner

If the mouth is very small compared to the size of the face and the other features, it indicates someone who is rather self-centered, perhaps hypercritical, and usually a loner. This mouth is often found in the obese, indicating one who overindulges himself or herself by eating rather than by seeking emotional satisfaction in other ways. It indicates deprivation at some level of life and overindulgence in another, as the other features of the face may reveal. Usually the person with such a mouth will have a rich fantasy life and prefer to be alone with his or her thoughts than to be out in the world babbling with others. However, once these people can be persuaded to communicate, they often have interesting ideas and remarkably acute insight into others. The problem is that they are fault-finders, and they become set in their views and extremely intolerant of others' foibles. Often they prefer pets to people, and it is usually through a hobby that they get involved with others, if at all. This mouth often also indicates low vitality and marginal health, conditions that tend to isolate even further. Take into consideration that this individual needs to think of himself or herself as just about perfect, and this requires a great deal of suppression of human desires and impulses. So, although small-mouth individuals may appear weak, even meek, they often are capable of great acts of will and very rigid opinions and consequently are somewhat dangerous to cross swords with.

Because the mouth tends to enlarge as we age, the person with a small mouth in youth sometimes is able to emerge more as he or she gets older, but the tendency to criticize and carp is rarely dissipated. However, these people are often hard and determined workers who achieve whatever goal they set for themselves.

2. SPECIAL MOUTHS

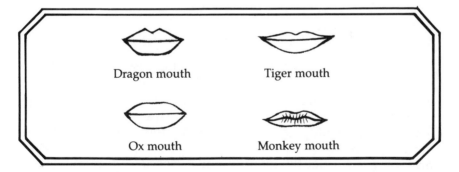

Dragon mouth

Tiger mouth

Ox mouth

Monkey mouth

There are four special mouths, each relating to an animal type. When you encounter one of these mouths, you are usually meeting a remarkable and fascinating personality.

Dragon Mouth. The one with such a mouth is extremely fortunate. The lips are full and the corners are clear; the lips are of good color. The outline of this mouth is slightly square and very definite. It is a clear, mobile mouth and indicates a good life, a robust personality, one who is also even tempered and kind.

Tiger Mouth. This mouth is so large that its owner can almost put his or her fist into it. It is large and broad, with large lips. However, it closes well and has good form and outline. The owners of such mouths are usually powerful people. They have high status, a rich long life and lots of money.

Ox Mouth. This mouth is also large, but the lips are thick and straight. It indicates someone who is basically pleasant, with a warm personality. These people have nice lives filled with peace and calm, enjoying good fortune.

Monkey Mouth. The lips are long and thin and have lots of lines around the middle. These people are not really misers, but they are very careful with money. They do enjoy long, healthy lives and are very reproductive.

GUIDELINES

The mouth represents the personality—the emotional, Yin side of the nature. The mouth often betrays facets of the individual that other features do not reveal.

Evaluate the mouth according to its size in relation to other features, its mobility, its definite outline, the fullness or thinness of the lips and the basic shape. Observe how the mouth is held— firm, relaxed, slightly open, tightly closed—as a key to the expression of the personality in life.

PART FOUR

THE SEVEN MINOR FEATURES

RANGE AND LIMITATIONS

Although the following features are considered "minor," they are by no means unimportant. The Seven Minor Features—forehead, undereye area, cheekbones, laugh lines, jawbone, chin and philtrum (the groove between the nose and mouth)—are lesser only in that they form a background for the major features. Of the Five Major Features each represents a potential—what you can do with a particular area of your life. The Seven Minor Features, on the other hand, represent directing forces that may strengthen or limit your potential but are to a great extent beyond your control. The Minor Features are compelling in that they shape the direction of your potential.

When your position point falls on one of the major features, you usually find yourself shaping your own life; when one of the minor features is involved, circumstances seem to control you.

Three of the minor features—forehead, cheekbones, and chin—are mountains of the face and should be prominent. These mountains support the major mountain, the nose, and it is advantageous if they are less prominent than the nose and do not crowd it too much. In other words, the desirable situation is for the mountains to create a balanced terrain with the nose as the peak.

As mountains, these features and also the jawbone partake of the nature of the cosmic energy Yang—the positive, masculine energy. They are all bony features that depend on the structure of the underlying bone for their prominence and shape.

The three remaining minor features—philtrum (the groove from the nose to the upper lip), undereye area and laugh lines around the mouth—are fleshy formations of the face and partake of the nature of the cosmic energy Yin—the receptive, feminine energy.

The qualities represented by the Seven Minor Features are:

> forehead—character
> cheekbones—power
> jawbones—status
> chin—strength
> philtrum—life force
> undereye—fertility
> laugh lines—longevity

We start with the four Yang features and then go on to the ones with the nature of Yin.

I

THE FOREHEAD

CHARACTER

The forehead represents character—the Yang, intellectual part of the nature. The forehead thus tells what one brings from one's background: education and parental guidance, principles that have been instilled, ability to make judgments and values that are lived by.

The forehead represents the planet Mars; its color is best pinkish, and it is beneficial if the forehead glows, if it's lightly shiny. Forehead lines, in general, are favorable (see page 196).

The forehead occupies the entire First Station of the face and so is concerned with youth, the first third of life. Its position points are 15 to 30, the years of youthful endeavor, when character is most decisive in what the life work and family situation will become. The forehead holds the significant Pathway of Heaven (Position Points 16, 19, 22, 25) and includes the Shrine of the Seal of Approval. The Palaces of Achievement, Parents, Friends and Siblings, Transfer (travel), Happiness and Good Fortune are on the forehead, indicating the variety of youthful experience and the way character is shaped by family, education and effort.

The forehead occupies the space from the hairline at the top of the face to the middle of the eyebrows—the upper ridge of the eye bone—and from hairline to hairline across the face. Keep in mind that the shape of the forehead decides the shape of the hairline, not the other way round, and the hair should not invade the territory of the forehead. In fact, it is advisable to ignore the shape of the hairline for the present and concentrate instead on the structure of the forehead itself. (Various types of hairlines and their meaning are discussed under Patterns of Hair Growth, page 200.)

Evaluate the forehead from several aspects. Is it bony or flat? High or low? What is its basic shape?

Forehead Bones

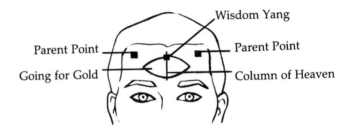

It is advantageous to have prominent bones in the forehead, and there are certain areas of the forehead where prominent bone structure indicates a special destiny and importance in the individual.

Wisdom Yang. A prominent bone at the top of the forehead is considered a mark of high intellectual prowess. If the entire area is prominent, it is called Going for Gold, indicating a drive for high achievement.

The Column of Heaven. This is a ridge of bone running down the middle of the forehead through Position Points 16, 19, 22 and 25, the Pathway of Heaven. Those with such a bone prominent are darlings of the gods and will produce some great achievement.

The Parent Bones. These are prominences at the Parent Points—Points 17 and 18—also called the Sun and the Moon Points, near the top of the forehead to each side of the Pathway of Heaven. Prominences here indicate powerful intellect, a strong, good influence from the parents and much wisdom.

Forehead Height

The forehead can usually be described as high, medium or low. A high forehead shows a good relationship with parents. In Chinese tradition, the eldest child usually has a high forehead and usually gets the most help from parents. If a child is not the eldest and has a high forehead, this person will usually have to take care of the parents while he or she is still young.

A medium-high forehead indicates good family background and good intellectual development. A low forehead indicates a poor start in life, with little help from parents and perhaps trouble in getting an education. Otherwise this person may have mental or emotional problems.

BASIC SHAPE

The basic shape of the forehead from the front view may be squarish, round or pointed.

Square

If the forehead is both high and square, it indicates a good intellectual ability and excellent values, with fine family background and good mental powers. However, it may be hard to maintain a good marriage relationship. If it is very high and very square, it implies early widowhood.

If the forehead is low and square, it indicates one who has probably had a poor start in life but has strong practical abilities and good character and will make the most of his or her innate abilities.

If the forehead is medium-high and square, it indicates one of sound intellect, good practical instincts and the background and education to achieve success in the middle positions.

 Rounded

A high and rounded forehead with no angles indicates a peaceful nature and a person who is probably not very aggressive or ambitious. This is an individual with a good background and pleasant childhood but perhaps not stimulated enough to develop intense interests and the desire for achievement.

If the forehead is low and rounded, the person often gets off to a poor start, but if the other features so indicate, he or she can get into a position of security in later life.

If the forehead is rounded and medium high, the person is often content with an average life and does not make much effort to change the condition into which he or she was born.

 Pointed

A narrow, pointed forehead is commonly seen on a Fire type. If it is high, this forehead signals a spirit of adventure. If it is low, it indicates impulsiveness and poor intellectual powers.

SLANT

As seen from the side, the slant of the forehead—straight, domed, sloping or bulging—is another indicator of character and aptitudes.

 Straight

If the forehead is high and straight—that is, flat from the side view and coming right down from the hairline to the brow bone—the individual has strong character and intellectual power but may become set in her or his views at an early age and hesitate to change with the times.

If the forehead is straight but also low, it means the individual has to work hard in youth for everything he or she gets, with little help from family.

 Domed

If the forehead is domed—rounded and full from the side view—it indicates a strong character and a sense of adventure, with an ability to make adjustments in life as events require change.

 Sloping

If the forehead slopes—is slanted back from the brow bone— it indicates a kind of basic restlessness, someone who is adventurous and has a reckless manner.

 Bulging

If the forehead bulges at the hairline, it indicates an excess of drive and intellectuality that may be out of balance with reality but also may foretell high achievement.

GUIDELINES

The forehead represents character—what a person receives from the family, background, education—and also one's relationship with parents. Evaluate the forehead by its boniness, height, basic shape and slant. Keep in mind that the forehead is a mountain and should be prominent.

II

THE CHEEKBONES

POWER

The cheekbones, too, are mountains of the face and part of the bony structure, and thus partake of the nature of the positive, masculine cosmic energy Yang. They represent power—in business and public life but also in marriage and family setup. A balance of power is needed for success in human relationships as well as in world and national affairs.

The cheekbones are called Great Yang. Their position points (46 and 47) are the Summit and the Crest. They support the major mountain, the nose, the Throne of the Emperor and the Peak of Perfection. There should be balance among these mountains, so the cheekbones are best not too close to the nose; they should not crowd it nor be so large that they dominate it. Each mountain should stand apart for greatest power.

The cheekbones comprise two parts—the knobs or terminals of the cheekbones below the eye in the middle of the cheek, and the base—the bone that connects the cheekbone to the eye bone. In the ideal situation of power, both the base and the knobs are strong. The places where the cheekbones connect with the eye bone at each side are called the Sun Bones. There are two, but they are considered as one and are one of the three important Yang bones of the face—Wisdom Yang, Great Yang and the Sun Bones. It is helpful to have prominences at these junctures.

In general, the knobs of the cheekbones represent the display or exertion of power and the base represents the authority to back up that power.

Strong cheekbones, both base and knobs, are required for any career that puts the individual into a post of authority and are especially helpful in military or government positions, theater, sports and medicine. In personal relationships, the partner with the stronger cheekbones (and supporting mountains) will rule the roost or try to, and that person will become the dominant spouse and dominant parent.

Basically, when you are looking at cheekbones, there are five types you encounter frequently.

 ## Strong Base with Strong Bone—Authoritative

This is the ideal cheekbone for one who rises to a high position in life because of authority and the power to make oneself felt. This cheekbone shows a person of prestige and power but also someone who is hard to live with. In family life, this person may be too authoritative and demanding for easy communication. If the jawbone and chin are also strong, this person may find it necessary to live alone. Although this cheekbone is useful for success in public life and career, the owner may be too powerful, domineering, willful and proud to share life intimately with another. This is particularly true of women who become superstars of the theater, politics and business but who wisely do not attempt to share their personal lives with another.

High and Round Without a Strong Base—Willful

These cheekbones also show someone who is difficult to handle. They show someone with power but lacking the authority to back it up. If these cheekbones are also close to the nose, it indicates one who wants to rule but doesn't gain control and is put down constantly by those in power. This individual may become the big fish in a little pond or may turn rebellious because of the urge to be felt in spite of a lack of authority.

High and Square with Strong Base—Bossy

Again, this is not a promising situation for getting along in family life, but for those who are in positions of authority at work, it indicates an ability to exert control and authority and to make others follow orders.

 Flat—Easygoing

These belong to the easygoing—those people who are comfortable to be with, make soft bosses and take things as they are in family life without too much struggle or attempts at discipline. Unfortunately, these people do not reach a high position in life because power does not appeal to them, and they feel unable to control others, as well. They are not, however, happy working for others under whose power they must fall and often end up self-employed.

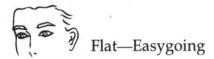 Narrow and Close to the Nose—Stubborn

If these cheekbones are not too close to the nose and not too prominent and in balance with the other mountains, they can bring the person to a powerful position without much effort. If the space between the cheekbones is very narrow and they are very close to the nose, these people become hard to deal with—unkind, selfish and unwilling to compromise.

GUIDELINES

When you are looking at the cheekbones, observe both the base and the knobs.

Relate the cheekbones to other mountains—the nose, the forehead and the chin. The chin and the forehead support the cheekbones, and the cheekbones should not crowd or dominate the nose.

Cheekbones show power in family life as well as in public life. In a couple, the one with the more prominent cheekbones will be the dominant partner and the dominant parent.

III

THE JAWBONES

STATUS

The jawbones represent status—the position one achieves in life. The jawbones partake of the masculine, active cosmic energy Yang. Some boniness and prominence are desirable, but the jawbones should be in balance with the rest of the facial structure and should not be too prominent.

The position points of the jawbones (Points 74, 75) are those of maturity, and the jawbones, like the cheekbones, often become more prominent in later years as the bony structure of the face becomes more pronounced. This is especially true if the jawbone is basically strong. If, however, it is naturally weak, it may be further weakened in age by loss of teeth and loss of bone. In the first situation, high status becomes more pronounced; in the second, the person may lose position with age.

The jawbones are most prominent at the lower, outer corners of the face. In a square face, these corners may be almost on the same level as the chin. In a triangular face, the jawbone tends to slope down from these corners to a pointed chin; however, the effect can also be rounded, so the jawline seems smooth and not at all bony.

In observing the shape of the jaw, keep it distinct from the chin—each has its own identity and meaning, even though these features support each other and eventually must also be related in evaluating the face.

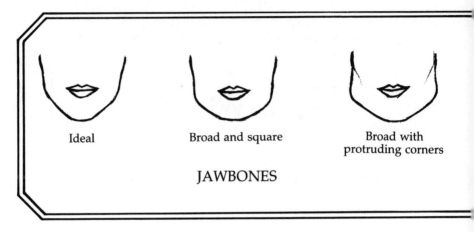

Ideal   Broad and square   Broad with
                                          protruding corners

JAWBONES

There are six types of jawline that you will commonly encounter, and each has its own relevance to status in life.

The Ideal Jawline—The Self-Sufficient

Ideally—that is, ideally for status in life—the jawline is firm and well molded, about equal in width to the forehead and neither short nor long; it is rounded, so that the bones are not too prominent and are slightly squared at the corners for a distinctive shape. Such a jaw indicates a self-sufficient and accomplished person who has balance in life and success, who can make a place in the world and win respect and position. Much of the value of this jawline and the ability to sustain position in later life depend upon the quality of the chin—strength.

Broad and Square—The Striver

This jawline indicates one who will be stubborn, self-centered and proud and will struggle to achieve a high position in life— and probably succeed. However, the very stubbornness of the jaw may defeat some of the gains, and this person may be lonely in the later years, isolated by his or her own status.

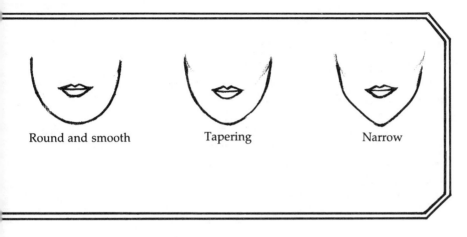

Round and smooth   Tapering   Narrow

Broad with Protruding Corners—
The Militant

This is a jaw that is so wide that the sides of the jawbone are visible from the back of the head. This represents a hard and domineering nature, one who will reach a high position in the military but who in public or business life tries to usurp power. This individual wants to be at the top and often makes it. His or her ambitions are not in a social or cultural field but rather in more disciplined businesses and professions. It is not wise to try to contend with anyone with this jawline. This individual seeks domination and will win or break you. It is better to avoid confrontations.

Round and Smooth—Secure

People with this round, smooth jawline are often born into a comfortable life and maintain their security, comforts and upper-middle position throughout their lives. This jawline shows a good family, a nice home, a pleasant disposition and a basically secure position in life. It also indicates one who does not aspire to rise very high and is never in danger of sinking very low. This pleasant sinecure may not be exciting, but it promises an easy life and a stable maturity.

Tapering Jaw—Narcissistic

Usually this jaw goes with the oval face, the admired face of beauty in women. It often promotes success and a rise in status, usually through the admiration and influence of others—a rise that does not take much effort on the part of the owner of this jawline. It makes for a gratifying youth and possibly middle years, but it tends to be less fortunate for the later period of life, bringing weakness of some kind, dissatisfaction or health problems that can mean a loss of status or an inability to enjoy the position one has attained.

Narrow Jaw—Disappointed

The narrow jaw, often tapering to a small chin, is a sign of weakness in health rather than in character (for the forehead is often correspondingly strong). Whatever good qualities for achievement and success this individual has are often lessened by the weakness of health or lack of stamina in the mature years, so that the desired position is never quite realized, or if it is achieved, will not be sustained. Somehow this jaw does not properly nourish the position desired by the person, and this can result in a disappointing life.

GUIDELINES

It is best for status to have a firm, somewhat prominent and well-molded jawline. Either too much or too little here can make an important difference. If it is too prominent, the individual may achieve status but be lonely. If there is too little, any status may be hindered by weakness in maturity.

Status, shown by a firm jawline, is increasingly important in the later years, when it can provide security and comfort.

THE CHIN

STRENGTH

The chin, the lowest part of the face, is another mountain. It represents strength. A knobby chin gives the stamina needed for sustained vitality throughout life and into old age. Position Point 71 dominates the chin—it indicates how hard you must work in life and whether you will have the stamina and vitality to continue being active in old age.

The position points of the chin are those of maturity. The Palaces of the Household, representing the reserves of vitality to meet the needs of later years, also occupy this area.

In observing the chin, look for its shape—rounded, pointed, squarish—and also for its knobbiness or flatness.

 The Ideal Chin—Stamina

This chin has good form and is also prominent. It is rounded at the sides but slightly squarish at the tip, firm and in good proportion to other mountains of the face. If one has such a chin, it denotes a strong, healthy life, with stamina persisting into maturity and vigorous children and grandchildren.

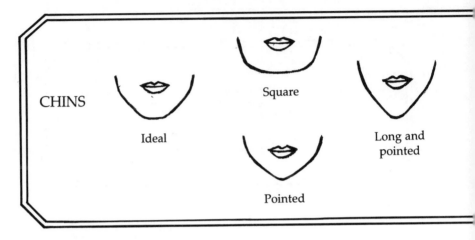

CHINS

Ideal

Square

Pointed

Long and
pointed

Square Chin—Fighter

A chin that is very square and firm indicates one who has an excess of strength, in fact one who is stubborn and a fighter. The owner of this chin comes at life full tilt and tends to be rather unyielding. Although such a person is strong physically, this is not necessarily a chin that wins support from others and thus it may be alienating, particularly in old age.

Pointed Chin—Vacillator

This chin is associated with narrowness of viewpoint and also with a vacillating will that often cannot stand up to others or to the vicissitudes of life itself. The owner of this chin may be too amenable in human relationships, forever giving in and giving out, and also may show weakness in health in maturity.

Long, Pointed Chin—Domineering

With a long, pointed chin (often seen in the diamond-shape face), the individual has a tendency to dominate others, especially in maturity, and may also be a gossip and a bit of a troublemaker.

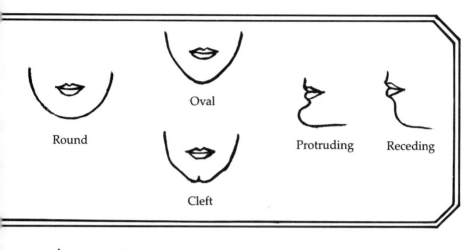

Round   Oval   Protruding   Receding

Cleft

Round—Politic

With this round chin, an individual may be much too prone to being politic, failing to show strength in dealing with others and taking things too easily. It indicates a kind of weakness rather than strength, and although the life may be of average length or longer, it will not be much fun, for this individual does not demand enough of self or others.

Oval—Petulant

This chin often provides enough strength for youth and middle age, but in old age, there tends to be weakness and a kind of petulance that diminishes strength. This chin is not promising for children, who are a source of strength in old age.

Cleft Chin—Immature

This is a sign of an adventurer, someone who remains immature, with the heart of a child, and who never settles down.

 Protruding Chin—Pugnacious

This is the chin of one who is perhaps too strong and often belligerent; such a person may be pugnacious and prefer to fight rather than work for what he or she gets. This may complicate his or her existence. However, the strength is there for a satisfying life if other mountains are prominent.

Receding Chin—Manqué

This indicates one who is somehow deprived of strength, whose aspirations are unfulfilled. The receding chin exposes the underside of the chin and thus is one of the Five Exposures, each of which is individually unfortunate although all five together are helpful. The strength of this person has no staying power and often is not able to sustain family relationships that give endurance in the later years. This person often comes up a loser unless other features are compensating.

GUIDELINES

The chin is the lowest part of the face and has much to do with the stamina and strength that carry over into a robust old age, though the strength shown by the chin is useful throughout life.

The chin is a mountain and should be related to the other mountains of the face.

V

THE PHILTRUM

LIFE FORCE

The philtrum is the groove from the nostrils to the upper lip. It partakes of the cosmic energy Yin and is a river, representing the drainage system of the face. It represents the life forces of productivity and sexuality, both in the procreative processes of life and also in the creative and productive spheres of work. It is the connecting channel from the nose, representing the male sex organ, to the mouth, representing the female sex organ, and so is an erotic feature.

Although the philtrum is little regarded currently in Western culture, it was considered an erogenous zone by the ancient Greeks; the word *philtrum* derives from the same root as *philter*, a love potion; *philanthropy*, love of giving; *philanderer*, a male flirt; and also *philately*, now the term for stamp collecting but originally meaning love of tax exemption.

The philtrum is a fascinating feature to observe because of the variety of forms it can take and also because few people are aware of it or understand its meaning and so are not self-conscious about it. The philtrum gives important insight into the sexual drive (or lack of it) and the productivity of the person in generating the fruits of life. The philtrum ideally is one inch long. This indicates that sexual stamina will endure throughout life.

Point 51 on the philtrum is called the Center of Life, referring to the productive energy often displayed at age fifty, an age when both men and women tend to get a new lease on life, renew their sexual prowess and often start a new affair or even a new marriage or somehow regenerate their productivity through a new career or other fresh start. It often is the age at which the first grandchild is born.

- If this groove is very deep, it shows one who is very sensual and lavishly productive.
- If it is well formed, it grants a vital, long-lasting sex life and the prospect for many children.
- If it is flat or shallow, it indicates one whose interests are likely to be engaged elsewhere rather than in sexual activity—one whose productivity in work and life may be slight.
- A flat or poorly formed philtrum or one that seems to vanish as it approaches the upper lip is not productive in business and does not attract a beneficial clientele in any line of work. It is human nature to be attracted to those whose life force is powerful, even if the individual is not an object of overt sexual interest.
- A deep, well-shaped philtrum, on the other hand, attracts business to those who deal with the public in any way—salespeople, greeters, show people and so on.

Flared—Vibrant Life Force

The top of the philtrum is narrow and the groove flares as it nears the upper lip. The groove is relatively deep and clearly defined, and also mobile. This is considered the best type, promising productivity, a steady metabolism, sexual energy and several children.

Narrowing—Restrained Life Force

This philtrum is wide at the top but narrows as it approaches the upper lip. If it is of slight depth, it restrains productivity. The person is only mildly fertile—having a single child or none—and is moderate in sexual desire.

Straight and Narrow—Restricted Life Force

With this philtrum, the individual may be restricted in love life and productivity and may produce only one or two children. However, if the groove is deep and well formed, the prospects for productivity are greater.

Flat or Disappearing—Diminished Life Force

If the philtrum is flat or loses its formation as it nears the upper lip, it is not productive and shows a diminishing life force in the later years. This person is often one who seems to lose out at age fifty.

GUIDELINES

Observation of the philtrum can be a fascinating aspect of face reading. It indicates the life forces of productivity and sexuality and is very significant in choosing a mate or any kind of partner.

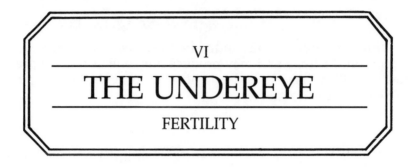

VI

THE UNDEREYE

FERTILITY

The area under the eye is the feature that reveals fertility—the number of offspring, the quality of the children and also, in a fashion, sexual desirability, because we are attracted to those who are fertile. This area is called the sleeping silkworm because, when it is slightly full and pale, it resembles the silkworm in the cocoon. This area also holds the Palaces of Offspring, the area one checks for the number of children one will have.

Note that there may be some confusion about the aspects of fertility and productivity represented by the undereye area as contrasted with the philtrum. Basically, the philtrum represents the life force of sexual desire and indicates the potential for having children. The undereye area shows fertility, sexual desirability—the number of children one actually has. Represented by the philtrum is the productivity of creation; the undereye represents the fruits, the results of creativity. The philtrum shows sexual activity; the undereye area, the children that result from that activity.

The desirable form of the undereye area is slightly full and light in color—an indication of sexual desirability, abundance of healthy offspring and normal sensuality. If the area is dark and sunken, it indicates barrenness and a downbeat, pessimistic view

188

of life—deprivation of sensual fulfillment. However, in all cultures, the presence of undereye shadows suggests one who goes to bed but not to sleep—either because of carnal pleasures or insomnia. In either case, shadows here are not considered favorable by the ancient Chinese, who believed in moderation in all things.

Note, too, that today's scientists suggest that many characteristics of the undereye area are hereditary and not necessarily an indicator of dissipation or poor metabolism. For example, pads of fat under the eye, becoming to the young and often later turning into bags that are mistakenly read as a sign of dissipation, can be an inherited trait that can appear without any hard living. They can be treated with cosmetic surgery if, in later years, one appears too much the bon vivant. Some ethnic groups normally have dark round-the-eye coloring that has nothing to do with metabolism. Puffiness around the eye can, however, indicate metabolic disorder.

The undereye area is very sensitive to day-to-day and over-the-lifetime change, just as is fertility. This area often reflects in women the stages of the menstrual cycle, and women on hormone contraceptives sometimes show the fullness and glow in the undereye area deceptively characteristic of the pregnant woman.

There are four types of undereye area to observe:

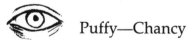 ### Slightly Full and Pale—The Fecund

This is the ideal condition for fertility. The area is slightly full, not flat, and the color is light and unshadowed and has a soft, dewy glow; it is not dry or wrinkled. This holds the promise for healthy offspring and sensual pleasures, along with fecundity in the areas of life that assure the provident care and nurturing of the young.

Puffy—Chancy

Too much undereye fullness due to pads of fat or puffiness due to water retention produces a negative situation for offspring and general fertility. Indicated are a weak constitution, little sexual stamina and a tendency to have accidents. If the eyes are protruding, even bulging, it helps the situation, for here we find one with fecundity, a willingness to take chances and a kind of bravery that meets life's challenges ably. This person may have many children and also may be fertile in imagination and in ways of producing the means of living. He or she may be a gambler, sometimes with the result that the offspring live chancy lives.

Flat with Good Color—Low Fertility

This is not a good sign for fertility. The one whose undereye area is flat with good color can have one or two healthy children, but the life as a whole will not be fruitful. This is because the owner of this formation tends to be cold and narcissistic, letting himself or herself be loved rather than being loving. There is something materialistic and self-centered about the flat sleeping silkworm indicative of those who have children not as an extension of love but to guarantee an inheritance, fulfill a marriage contract, prove oneself or gratify the ego. However, in Western values, the flat, clear area is considered cosmetically desirable. If the color is not good—if it is shadowed—fertility is further inhibited.

Sunken or Shadowed—Unfulfilled

If this area is hollow or darkly shadowed, it shows metabolic problems, one who is infertile or one who does not want children or is unhappy with children and generally negative about life. This is a condition that can occur after one has produced children or can improve if habits or physical disorders are corrected. Shadows under the eye, as we have seen, are also considered an indicator of one who is sexually overindulgent, even if not highly fertile, and so may appear desirable.

GUIDELINES

The desirable condition is slight fullness with light color and a gentle glow.

The negative qualities are flat, sunken or hollowed, dark shadows or other discoloration.

The condition of this area is subject to day-to-day and over-the-lifetime change.

VII

THE LAUGH LINES

LONGEVITY

The laugh lines, called *Fa Ling*, run from the corners of the nose along the sides of the mouth. They represent longevity and are also indicators of vitality and good health. These lines are present from birth—they give expression to the mouth—but they are better not etched there (present when the mouth is in repose) till after age forty or beyond. If they appear earlier, they are considered somewhat unfavorable, although executive men and women often show such lines in their thirties.

What can we learn from the laugh lines? That one who laughs a lot lives longer? Long laugh lines indicate a long, robust life if they do not curve into the corners of the mouth. The position points of the laugh lines are 56 and 57. If one survives beyond the age of fifty-five or fifty-six, represented by these points, one will probably live a lot longer.

Today in the West, a normal life span of seventy to seventy-three years is to be expected. The Chinese, however, considered living to a great age to be living beyond that. One of the valued attributes of life is that one should live to see not only one's grandchildren but one's great- and great-great-grandchildren. A shorter-than-normal life span, if one is indicated by these lines, shows somewhat less than the allotted three score and ten (seventy), while a great old age takes you well into the nineties or to one hundred.

The laugh lines are related to sensuality and power, for they separate the cheeks (power) from the mouth area (personality). Those who live long have a balance between these attributes.

Ideally for health and long life, the laugh lines should be long and curved. Paintings and drawings by the ancient Chinese show saints and sages with long mustaches that curve out slightly at the bottom. These follow the curve of the ideal laugh lines, indicating not only wisdom and balance but also that these sages were full of years as well as wisdom.

There are five basic kinds of laugh lines:

Very Long, Curving Down and Then Out

If the laugh lines are very long and curve down and then out at the bottom, you will be a longevity star, seeing five generations of your descendants.

Long and Curved Out

If the lines are long and continue to curve out below the mouth, this indicates a long life with vitality and much activity in later years.

Average Length and Curved

If the lines are of average length, reaching only to the outer corners of the mouth, and if they are curved out, you will live an average life span and will enjoy good health and well-being.

Long and Curved In

If the laugh lines are long and curve in below the mouth, it indicates a long life but possible loneliness at the end.

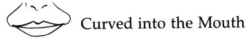 Curved into the Mouth

If the laugh lines curve into the corners of the mouth, it indicates poverty or poor health in old age and possibly starvation or deprivation of another kind.

Good nutrition in the early years, influencing the prospect of retaining sound teeth and not suffering bone loss in the later years, is one way to maintain a happy curve on the laugh lines and perhaps live longer and better. The condition of these lines, along with that of the whole lower face, is greatly dependent on good health, as is happiness in the later years.

GUIDELINES

The laugh lines are present from birth but are better not etched in the face till after age forty. If they are long and curved, they support long life.

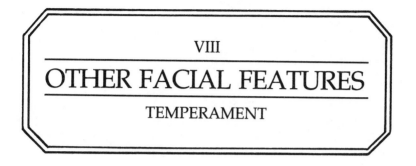

VIII

OTHER FACIAL FEATURES

TEMPERAMENT

In addition to the Five Major Features and the Seven Minor Features there are lesser facial features—lines, markings, hair type and patterns of hair and beard growth—that have meaning in face reading and help bring out nuances of the individual's nature. These can often give a quick insight into another's temperament. They also throw added light on the quality of any feature with which they are associated.

1. FACIAL LINES

In addition to the laugh lines around the mouth, there are other facial lines that have significance. These are the horizontal lines on the forehead, vertical lines between the brows (frown lines), lines at the corners of the eyes (crow's feet) or around the eyes; and some unusual lines, such as a line running down the nose, across the root of the nose, under the eyes and so on. Lines around the upper lip appear sometimes in the elderly. All these lines help interpret the feature upon which they appear and have significance in the life pattern of the person you observe.

One line

Two lines

Three lines

Horizontal forehead lines: In general, these lines are considered fortunate. If there is one horizontal forehead line and it is high, crossing the forehead at Position Point 16 (Middle Sky) or 19 (Court of Heaven), it can help bring success. Sometimes a line starts at one of these points and runs across one side of the forehead only. The side it appears on (right, Yin, or left, Yang) will indicate the nature of the success.

If there is one horizontal line and it is low, crossing at Point 22 or Point 25, it is considered less fortunate and limits one's success. Again, if the line starts in the middle and runs to one side, it indicates limitations in the Yin (right) or Yang (left) activity.

Two horizontal lines are considered extremely favorable. They endow extremely high intelligence and indicate a self-achiever and self-starter.

If one has three horizontal lines, one needn't be bright and clever. Life is kind to this person; good fortune falls in his or her lap. This person has it made from infancy—a good position in life and nice things come without hard work.

Vertical lines between the brows. Two vertical lines—the so-called frown lines—between the eyebrows are normal and considered fortunate. Three are even better. More than three are not so lucky, and a single line is unfortunate.

Two or three vertical lines show a fine intellect, great cultural endowment and perspicacity. More than three vertical lines between the eyebrows show a tendency to scatter one's forces and dissipate intellectual efforts. The person becomes a scatterbrain. A single vertical line between the brows is called the suspending needle and augurs disappointment. The person with such a line is likely to get off to a brilliant start but expectations are not fulfilled. This person is often beset by many tensions and pressures, although by nature he or she is likely to be intellectually superior. Writers often have this suspending needle. So do others whose work produces anxiety.

Lines around the eyes. These lines appear in the outer corners of the eyes and sometimes on the upper and lower lids.

 Crow's feet. These are lines at the outer corners of the eyes, so-called because when there are three, which is common, they look like the track of a crow's foot. These lines are in the Palaces of Marriage and indicate the number of marriages (left eye) and extramarital affairs (right eye) that will be indulged in. Normally—and for happy marriage—these areas should be flat and clear. Many crinkles here, especially in the youthful, indicate sexual overindulgence and someone who may be a poor bet for a long relationship.

Horizontal lines on lower and upper lid. Normally there is a crease in the upper lid, and this is fortunate. More than one horizontal line above or below the eye is an indicator of a suspicious or watchful nature. If these lines are wavy, it shows generosity and a good nature.

Vertical lines in the lower lid. These are normal as one ages, but if three vertical lines, sweeping out toward the outer corner of the eye, appear in a man under thirty (this is an uncommon situation), they warn of one who will be hard on his children.

Other lines: A line down the middle of the nose shows one who will have to work hard for money and may be unable to earn much or hold onto it very long.

- A single horizontal line across the root of the nose on a man also indicates one who will be hard on his family.

- Sometimes vertical lines appear on the upper lip, and these indicate a self-centered, sometimes reclusive individual with a diminished reserve of health for old age.

2. MOLES, FRECKLES AND OTHER FACIAL MARKINGS

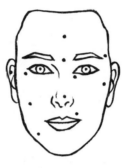

Hidden moles—moles on the body, particularly on the soles of the feet—are considered by and large fortunate. Moles on the face—exposed moles—may be both fortunate and unfortunate at the same time. Incidentally, if you have a mole on your face, you are said to have a corresponding mole on your body, and surprisingly often, this is true. Moles mark strong points. When they are hidden, this force is said to be under control. When the moles are exposed, the force is not under control.

Forehead moles. These are fortunate for career, negative for family life.

Two dragons clasping a pearl. This is a mole at Position Point 28 between the eyebrows. If it is light and bright in color or shiny, it is fortunate and indicates one who achieves a high position but who may also become very worldly and sophisticated.

A mole in the middle of the forehead, at Position Point 22, is a signifier of high position and achievement, but of one who may become too aggressive to stay married very long.

Eye-area moles. A mole at the outer tip of the eyebrow indicates much travel and movement in life but perhaps a lack of stability in domesticity. A mole just below the outer corner of the eye is the mole of the flirt or philanderer. It is considered attractive, romantic and sexy, but its owner may be fickle in love, even adulterous.

The weeping mole. This is found at the lower inner corner of the eye and is said to bring unhappiness, often because its owner has health problems.

Cheek moles. A mole high on the cheekbone toward the outer part of the face gives power and strength, but sometimes at the cost of good human relationships.

Society moles—moles on the lower cheek at the Society Points— show one who is fortunate and sociable but not always lucky at marriage, and perhaps somewhat unstable emotionally.

Lower face moles. A *gourmet mole*—at the outer corner of the upper lip—indicates one who enjoys good food and other good things of life and is friendly but who may be overly self-indulgent and difficult to please.

Matchmaker's Mole. A mole on the outer corner of the chin, called the Matchmaker's Mole, indicates a very colorful person, but one who is perhaps a busybody and tends to be somewhat interfering.

Ear moles. Ear moles in general are considered fortunate and promise high achievement, a good position in life and a fine family.

Nose moles. A mole on the tip of the nose, in a male, is said to give many healthy children.

Freckles. Freckles are considered friendly and the mark of one who is perhaps sexually indulgent.

Scars, birthmarks, blemishes. These are not considered fortunate. The skin should be unbroken, seamless. A scar at the position point for any year warns of hazards at that time of life. Birthmarks are also ill omens. Blemishes, especially those that leave scars, are considered unlucky.

3. PATTERNS OF HAIR GROWTH

Angular   Peach Blossom

High & Square   Temple Points

For good auspices, the hair should not grow too low behind the ears or at the temples, nor should it invade the territory of the forehead. When the hairline invades the forehead—meaning that hair is actually growing in the forehead area below the normal hairline—the person is suspected of low mentality or instability. This situation is comparatively rare and should not be confused with a low forehead.

- If the hairline is low, but does not invade the forehead, it is still a poor sign for the parents and the individual does not have an extremely long life.
- If the hairline is high, it shows a good relationship with parents.
- If the hairline is very high and very square, it is hard to keep a relationship in marriage and may mean widowhood.
- If the forehead is high and the hairline is uneven, this is not a problem. If the forehead is low and the hairline is ragged, it indicates complexities in the personality.
- If the hair grows to a point in the middle of the forehead, it indicates charm and flirtatiousness. In a woman this is called the Peach Blossom or the Peak of the Belle. In a man or a woman, it indicates one who is romantic, has many relationships and is good in money matters— capable, adventurous and creative though somewhat self-centered. In Western culture, this formation is called a widow's peak, indicating early widowhood, but in the Chinese tradition, it has no such meaning.
- Hair that grows in at points on the temples indicates one who is creative, artistic and alert, and although the personality is complex and hard for others to cope with

and understand, the individual has vision and creative spirit, and the formation is considered fortunate.
• If the hairline is extremely angular, it shows aggressive executive capacities and resourcefulness—one who is strongly career oriented, perhaps at the expense of family life.

 ## 4. BEARD PATTERNS

A beard that is not too coarse or bristly or too thin or fine indicates fine qualities in the character. The Chinese strive always for balance.

It is best when the beard has a clear pattern of growth, not reaching too high on the cheeks and with a clean outline (not ragged). The beard should grow evenly, not in whorls or with irregular thickness.

It is positive for sexual vitality for the beard to grow within the area of the philtrum, the groove from the nose to the upper lip. If a man affects a mustache, he decreases his fortune by shaving this area and exposing the philtrum. However, if the philtrum is flat or missing, a mustache helps keep this secret.

Allowing the beard to grow is a cosmetic aid for men with a poorly formed or receding chin.

5. THE HAIR

The hair on the head is not really a feature of the face, but it is visually so closely tied to the face that it becomes significant in face reading. The quality of the hair of the head and the beard are both significant.

The hair and beard partake of the nature of the cosmic energy Yin, the passive, receptive energy. The hair represents the condition of the blood, the nutrient of life. Hair that is shiny and smooth—that flows, so to speak—is considered a sign of good health and vitality. Hair is best when it is not too coarse or too abundant. Overly thick and coarse hair is said to indicate that the hair is stealing strength from the body; the blood is nourishing the hair at the expense of the living tissue. Nor should the hair be too fine or thin, for this indicates thin, weak blood.

In face reading, the hair is evaluated for its texture (coarse, fine), its abundance (thin, thick), its curliness or straightness, its color and gloss.

Texture

Ideally the hair is of medium texture and of medium abundance. It should be smooth and straight, but not too straight and flat; and it should be shiny but not oily. Such hair indicates a person with sound creative ideas and reasonable ambitions, one who will accomplish much in the middle years and have a happy old age.

If hair is coarse, the person is said to be impulsive, usually temperamental, active, aggressive, an achiever and often self-employed or involved in sports or the military.

If hair is very coarse, the person is tempestuous, with strong opinions, and becomes a powerful opponent.

Abundance

Too much hair, hair that is thick and bushy or very heavy, indicates a hard life. If the hair is very thick or overabundant, the person is overemotional, too strong and aggressive, and may lack more refined qualities. However, hair that is very coarse and thick is not a great problem if the person is also large boned and the body is powerful. But on a small-boned person, it indicates lack of balance. The person finds it hard to realize results or to accomplish much, and the promise of long life is diminished.

Fine hair indicates a sensitive and artistic nature, one who will be creative but perhaps overly sensitive and even timid, lacking the aggressiveness needed to achieve goals. However, this person is intelligent and has a fine character and an even temperament.

If hair is very thin, it indicates one who is shrewd but in whom vitality is diminished and who may become old before his or her time. If hair is very thin and flat, the person will be vain, love flattery and also be insecure and lacking in initiative.

Normal balding (hereditary balding) is considered a sign of intellectual growth but abnormal (patchy) balding at an early age is negative. Even in old age, it is considered better if hair merely thins and is not entirely lost.

Curliness

If the hair is curly, the person is bright, with good intellect but very fickle. If hair is very curly, it indicates self-indulgence, perhaps a lack of dependability and an irresponsible nature—one who is not very stable emotionally.

If hair has irregular curls, it indicates one who is temperamental. If hair is only slightly wavy, the tendency to irresponsibility is lessened considerably, although there is some tendency to sexual dalliance.

Very straight hair indicates one who is compassionate and perhaps insufficiently aggressive.

If hair is soft, bright and shiny, not too coarse or too fine and not overly oily and pleasantly fragrant, the person reaches high position and finds a good money situation.

Color

Hair color is preferably rich and strong, to show vitality and good health. If hair color is light and the hair is dry and lackluster, it indicates one who is temperamental, and the effect is negative for those close to the individual.

If hair grays early, it indicates a hard life ahead. Hair that grays gradually in the middle years is an indicator of achievement. Hair that is gray in old age is a mark of honor. If hair goes gray or white in youth and the color is regained in later years, it is considered a poor sign for the children, as if the renewal of youth in the parent sapped the offsprings' strength.

GUIDELINES

Evaluate the lesser features in terms of any feature they may be related to—forehead, nose, eyes, mouth, cheeks, chin—and also for their specific indications of temperament and the general fortunes of the person observed.

PART FIVE

HOW TO USE FACE READING

Face reading can provide unique insights into your own or another's nature, revealing potentialities and aptitudes, strengths and weaknesses. It can help you stage your life to make the best moves at the best time. It also permits you to make quick, everyday checks on your chances for success in any enterprise and provides a gauge of vitality and energies. You can use face reading as a guide to the propensities of others you pair up with in long or brief relationships, either personal or business, alerting you to the advantages and difficulties you assume when you enter into any kind of partnership. You can also use it to help others realize their potential and keep their energies up to par.

As previously mentioned, you can do this by proceeding in a step-by-step manner, analyzing all aspects of the face and features in the following order:

1. Discern the elemental type of the individual.
2. Evaluate the cosmic energies (active Yang, receptive Yin).
3. Check the Three Stations to see if they are balanced or if one is dominant.
4. Evaluate the Five Major Features, the Seven Minor Features and the lesser features for their indications.
5. Listen to the voice and observe the posture.
6. Check to see if the features exhibit the appropriate colors.
7. Check the position point for the fortunes of the current year and the thirteen middle points for a life reading.
8. Discern whether the individual has warmth, heart and inner glow.

Or you can immediately spot-check those characteristics that lead to success in career and personal relationships. Here, then, are the major points to look for in these areas of life activity.

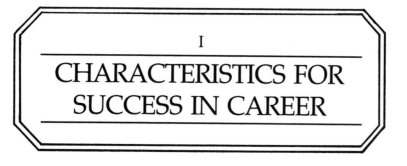

I

CHARACTERISTICS FOR SUCCESS IN CAREER

Certain indicators on the face are significant of a high level of success in whatever field the individual plans to enter. Perhaps the most outstanding signifier of success is a purplish circle at Position Point 28—The Shrine of the Seal of Heaven and the Star Point Purple Air. Good space, formation and color here indicates a darling of the gods.

Look also to the Yangs—the significant bones of the face:

The Column of Heaven. A vertical bone down the middle of the forehead through Position Points 16, 19 and 22 indicates brilliance.

Prominences at the Sun and Moon Points. Position Points 17 and 18, near the top of the forehead on the sides of the Pathway of Heaven, are also called the Parent Points. Bony protrusions here indicate great opportunity.

Wisdom Yang. A bony prominence at the top of the forehead indicates high intellect. When it bulges, it is called Going for Gold and indicates a great drive for achievement.

The Sun Bones. These appear at the temples where the cheekbones join the eye bone. Prominence and warm color here indicate potential for success.

Great Yang. Cheekbones prominent at base and knobs show one who will exercise great power.

1. INDICATORS OF POTENTIAL FOR WEALTH

There are many characteristics that indicate a potential for making money. Look for them in yourself, in a possible mate, partner or employer, or in anyone else involved in your accumulation of wealth.

- The pure Water type is very fortunate in making money. With characteristics of Water present in a mixed type, the potential is also fortunate. The direction of Water is toward wealth, and its Vitality is flexibility, so pure Water often gets wealthy with a minimum of effort. That is why he or she is so fortunate. This person realizes one factor in the ancient Chinese ideal of happiness—money without having to work hard for it. Characteristics of Water are a swarthy complexion, a round face and rounded features.
- The nose is the feature that shows the potential for wealth and how money will be handled. Look for a long, prominent aquiline nose with a pendulous tip or a prominent, well-rounded Sheep Nose, a nose with a fat Peak of Perfection and concealed nostril openings. Or the Dragon Nose, a nose that comes straight down from the forehead with no indentation at the root and a peak that is straight but rounded, with nostril flares close to the nose. Any nose with a fat round Peak of Perfection indicates an accumulation of money.
- The person with *all five* of the Five Exposures—eyes protruding, ears bent forward, nostrils exposed, teeth exposed and chin receding—can also become rich. However, these individuals enrich themselves; they will not necessarily enrich those with whom they enter into partnerships or for whom they act as agent. In fact, the results may be quite the contrary.
- Hair that is bright and shiny, neither too thick nor too thin and not oily but pleasantly fragrant, is another asset in moneymaking, for it gives a strong sense of values. It helps, too, in achieving wealth to have a voice that is deep and resonant, like a bell.
- For making money in real estate, look for rounded eyebrows and fatty prominences below the eyebrows (Palaces of Property).

- Indicators of gambling fortune are protruding eyes, protruding inner rim of the ear, wide mouth, square jaw.
- A person usually has to work hard for money if he or she has a nose that is flat at the bridge or if the forehead is low and square.

GUIDELINES

It is important to recognize your own assets and liabilities in money-making potential, but it is equally important to evaluate those of any person you employ or are employed by or who will act as your agent or with whom you enter into financial partnership. Bear in mind that you're the one who hopes to gain by the relationship—you do not wish merely to enrich another.

In addition to the money-making potential of any potential business partner, evaluate his or her character (forehead), wisdom (ears), intelligence (eyes) and other characteristics to be sure you are dealing with someone who will be honest as well as financially able.

2. INDICATORS OF HIGH POSITION

In every walk of life, there are certain people who are destined to rise to a high place.

- The pure Gold type is very fortunate in the reaching of high status, and these people are found in management positions. The characteristics of Gold are oblong face, the three stations balanced, and ivory complexion.
- Long ears that are set high are also indicative of a rise in status.
- Strong, well-shaped jawbones are a prime indicator of achieving status. It is helpful, however, if all the mountains—nose, forehead, cheekbones and chin—are also balanced.
- The Three Stations should be balanced.
- Look for cheekbones with a strong base and strong knobs.
- Look for a forehead that is high and squarish, with prominent bones.

- Look for a chin that is round but slightly square at the tip.
- Look for eyebrows that are high, smooth and well arched.
- Look for a mouth that is large and slightly squared.
- Hair should be smooth, silky, glossy, fine and flowing.
- A contained and composed manner indicates high status.
- Listen for a melodious voice.

It is negative for high position if:

- The head is small.
- The forehead is narrow.
- Lots of forehead wrinkles show.
- Eyebrows are close to eyes.
- The space between the brows is narrow, with vertical lines.
- Skin is thin and taut.
- Eyes lack glow.
- Nostrils are exposed.
- Mouth is small or doesn't close properly.

GUIDELINES

Consider how the high position in life is to be achieved. The pure Gold type achieves it with little effort, others through fame (eyebrows), showmanship or career effort. So in addition to the characteristics given here for status, examine the other features, read the thirteen middle points and look at the star-point area. Particularly consider the middle points on the nose—Sitting on Top of One's Age (44), Sitting on Top of One's Longevity (45).

3. INDICATORS OF SECURITY AND STABILITY

Security, rather than wealth or high position, is the goal of many people, although they are not, of course, mutually exclusive. Both money and position contribute to security.

- The person who is assured of much security and stability is the pure Earth type—squarish face, tan complexion,

prominent features; the Earth face is often heavily mus-
cled and the veins may stand out.
- The nose is best when it is prominent, with a rounded tip
  and a clear, firm form at the points of Age (44) and
  Longevity (45). The Root of the Mountain (Point 41) is
  clear.
- The jaw is very square or round and smooth.
- The chin is squared off.
- Cheekbones have a strong base and strong knobs.
- The mouth is wide, firm and slightly squared.
- The forehead is broad and square, with prominent bones.
- The philtrum is deep and clear.
- The undereye area is slightly full and light in color.
- There are one or two horizontal lines on the forehead, set
  between points 19 and 22.
- Eyebrows are long and straight, with a strong brow bone.
- Teeth are white and strong.

Negative for security are:

- Protruding eyes.
- Exposed nostrils.
- Short eyebrows.
- A flat bridge on the nose.
- Cheekbones that are narrow and close to the nose, with
  strong knobs but no base.
- Discoloration in the undereye area.
- Greenish coloring in skin.
- Receding chin.
- Small, deformed ear or ear with protruding inner rim.
- Small mouth.

GUIDELINES

Many of the factors concerned with wealth, achievement and
status also contribute to security, but note that the characteristics
of steadiness (stillness), not the activist characteristics, contribute
most to stability in career.

4. INDICATORS OF PROFESSIONAL ACUMEN

Wisdom is of value in many occupations, but it is a necessity in the professions. Wisdom differs from intelligence, which is shown in the eyes. For one thing, wisdom includes the aptitudes for deductive, inductive and logical reasoning, the ability to benefit from experience. Intelligence comes at any level, but wisdom also embraces intuitive faculties, imagination and the higher mind.

Wisdom is the Fortune of Wood, and the pure Wood type is extremely fortunate in the endowment of professional acumen. The Wood element is shown in the triangular face; broad, high forehead and narrow chin; olive (grayish-green) complexion and a tendency to prominent bony structure in the face, especially in the forehead. The field of expertise of Wood is the thinking professions—education, religion, sciences, government, law, publishing, the creative arts. Consequently, anyone who plans to go into a profession benefits from some Wood, and if you are seeking help from a professional, you benefit from the wisdom this element grants.

- Look for the long, large ear, set high and close to the head, with very long lobes—preferably the Buddha ear (with very long lobes).
- Look for a high bony forehead, especially for Wisdom Yang—a prominent bone at the top of the forehead indicating strong intellect.
- Look for clear well-shaped eyes, with adequate space between them and also a large space between the eyes and the eyebrows. Deep-set eyes are also an asset in the research areas of science and the arts.
- Look for a long straight nose—the thinker's nose.
- Cheekbones are best with a strong base and some strength in the knobs, though the latter should not be too prominent.
- A balanced mouth.
- Firm well-molded jawline.
- Strong knobby chin even if lower face is narrow.

Negative for professional acumen are:

- A low, narrow or pointed forehead.
- Pointed ear, no lobe.
- Small pupils.
- Upturned nose.
- Very thick lips.

GUIDELINES

Usually to succeed in a profession the individual needs a good family background, extensive education and fine character, so the forehead is the key to this quality of Wisdom. Intelligence (eyes), large long ears, an ethical nose, and well balanced mouth also help reasoning powers.

Indicators of a long life (see page 217) are also an asset in professional life in which it takes years to get preparation and requisite experience.

5. SIGNATURES OF SUCCESS IN VARIOUS LINES OF WORK

In addition to the features that indicate a propensity for one or another direction in career, there are certain markers that indicate a predilection for a particular work activity. Here are some of them:

Theater

- prominent cheekbones, strong base and bone
- arched eyebrows
- large, luminous eyes
- strong, square jawline

Sports and Military

- square face
- thick eyebrows that turn up at the corners

- wide mouth
- strong jawbones
- short eyelashes

Law

- high forehead
- sharp-focused eyes
- thin upper lip
- full lower lip

Medicine

- large, luminous eyes
- prominent cheekbones
- buddha ears

Writing

- high forehead
- luminous eyes
- suspending needle (vertical line between eyebrows)

Real Estate

- fat pouches under eyebrows (Palaces of Property)
- rounded eyebrows

Research and Education

- oblong face
- greenish-gray coloring
- high forehead
- long ears

Creative Arts

- ruddy coloring
- inverted triangular face
- deep-set eyes

Advertising, Public Relations, Salesmanship

• high forehead
• wedge-shape brows
• strong cheekbones with strong knobs
• strong jaw and chin
• sharp, bright eyes
• ear with round top and no lobe
• conic-shape face

II

CHARACTERISTICS AFFECTING PERSONAL RELATIONSHIPS

In personal relationships, we think primarily of our life partner and our family, our friends and social group, but actually these personal relationships permeate every area of life—work, community activities, organizations to which we belong and attitude toward our institutions, politics and government, even world affairs.

Life is pleasant when we relate well to others; it can be hard, indeed, when through lack of understanding, relationships cause problems. Appreciating the goals of others and how our own needs relate to them can help smooth away many of the difficulties. Often, we are disturbed by others because they aren't like us or somehow don't measure up to our expectations. Through face reading, we can get to know others better and see what they are all about, how they differ from us and why they want things we don't care about—and also how to deal with such differences.

One of the basics of understanding is evaluating the elemental type. Some elements are compatible, some are helping to others and some are hindering. Because many of us are mixed types, it is usually possible to find compatible elements in another and stress these while minimizing the hindering effects of other elements.

As a get-acquainted measure, it is always helpful to analyze another person's ears. The ears show the kind of infant this person was, and they also show his or her life potential. Once we understand this, we can see how close to another we can come or how distant we must remain.

Another important clue is the forehead, which shows character, background and education. Some people have not been given a good start in life but have made a place for themselves; others came of good background with solid family support. We may expect too little of one, too much of another. In life, like often chooses like, but equally true is that opposites attract.

Look, too, to the cosmic energies. Some people choose to live altogether in the Yin (emotional) side of their nature, and for these individuals, life is often crisis after crisis. Others try to live too much in the Yang (rational) and seem cold and unsympathetic, martinets. A balance in the energies—emotional and cultural, work and rational—is needed by all to survive.

To determine compatibility, we need to check the other's vitality—his or her potential for strength and health as well as for long life. Look especially for heart, or inner glow, which can transform otherwise negative features into a positive effect.

And bear in mind that you are not looking for perfection. You are looking for another who is compatible. In understanding the quality of personal relationships, evaluate the longevity factors and hence the vitality. Then the indicators of sexual stamina and then the characteristics that bear on the role the other will play in your life—spouse, friend, travel companion and so on. You will have to make adjustments, but also consider that the other will have to make adjustments to you, too.

1. INDICATORS OF LONG LIFE AND VITALITY

Although the length of life is chiefly indicated in the laugh lines—they are best long and curved for a long life—other features of the face are also indicators of the longevity star and hence the one with vitality and stamina.

For a long, active life, look for some of these characteristics:

- The face is long, and the three stations are long and full.
- The jaw and chin are powerful.

- The skin is thick and elastic.
- The ears are thick and firm and set high, with long earlobes that turn inward. The bones behind the ear protrude, and after age 40, hairs grow in the ears.
- The brows are long and arched, with sufficient space between them. After age 40, long, colorful hairs stand up from the eyebrows.
- The Shrine of the Seal of Heaven (Point 28) is clear.
- The eyes are long and have a gentle glow.
- The nose is straight and prominent, and the tip is rounded.
- The philtrum is long and deep—if it is 1 inch long, the owner should live to be one hundred.
- The corners of the mouth turn up, and the lips are pinkish red.
- The voice is resonant and deep.

Also check the planet points for appropriate color, indicating good health—forehead, pink; eyes, bright; ears, light; nose, golden tan; mouth, rosy red.

The life span is shortened if all the following characteristics are present:

- The forehead is narrow and pointed.
- The eye bone is low, with eyebrows close to eyes.
- The eyebrows slant down.
- The eyes protrude and lack glow.
- The philtrum is short and shallow.
- The skin is very tight or very flabby, with greenish or bluish coloring.
- The lips are very dark and do not close properly.
- The ears are paper thin and soft, with no cartilage.
- The person sleeps with eyes or mouth open and the breathing pattern is tight.

GUIDELINES

A long life (and good health) is important in achieving much that one wants and bolsters the opportunities for achievement and enjoyment of one's fruits. However, do not upset yourself if you lack some or many of the characteristics that make for longevity. Few Westerners today have a very short life. The average life span is seventy or more years. A long life is considerably more than seventy.

2. INDICATORS OF SEXUALITY

In evaluating sexuality per se, look at the philtrum, the undereye area and the outer corners of the eyes.

- The philtrum is associated with the life force and shows sexual stamina and sexual desire, along with productivity.
- The undereye area shows the fertility—the results of sexual activity, the number and quality of the children.
- The corners of the eyes indicate fidelity—the number of marriages (left eye) and the number of extramarital affairs (right eye) are indicated by the lines in this area. One line or a clear area is desirable; three lines (crow's feet) are normal in later years; many crinkles here, especially at an early age, indicate sexual frivolity.

There are many other characteristics associated with sexual activity. Note that not all of these are positive—and too many of them indicate a tendency toward promiscuity. If you discover a great number in a single individual, you are likely to be observing a philanderer or a flirt, one who may not be a good bet as a life partner.

- light eyebrows with loose hairs
- deep laugh lines
- large mouth with full lips
- full or protruding eyes
- high cheekbones
- protruding ears
- upturned nose
- long nose that points down
- strong chin
- shadows under eyes
- tendency to keep the mouth open
- very thick or curly hair

- deep voice
- large head
- freckles
- highly arched brows
- laugh crinkles at the corners of the eyes
- deep philtrum
- warm and glowing position point

Negative for sexuality are:

- flat or disappearing philtrum
- hollowed or extremely dark undereye area
- thin, bony nose
- small, thin mouth
- thin, fine hair
- no beard growth in philtrum
- dull eyes
- lack of glow at position point, or discoloration

GUIDELINES

Indicators of a positive sexual drive are a deep, well-formed philtrum; full, light color in the undereye area, and smoothness at the outer corners of the eyes. The position point should also be warm and glowing.

3. CHOOSING A MARRIAGE PARTNER

Fortunately, everyone's image of the ideal mate is not the same. And some people have no interest in marriage. Others don't expect to get married once and forever, preferring instead to change partners from time to time. Some marry for money, position or security rather than for an active sex life and children. Basically, though, people who marry have similar goals—to enjoy an active sex life and to provide a home in which children can be nurtured, to enjoy the companionship of a life partner, to establish a background for social life and a base for community activities.

Women traditionally look for a good provider and protector for their children, someone who will offer security and status as well as companionship. Men traditionally want a good home-maker and mother for their children, a pleasant hostess and a cheerful companion.

The following factors at least cannot be ignored in choosing a desirable mate.

- When you are choosing a life partner, you must first recognize your own elemental type and that of your prospective mate and find at least some compatible elements.
- Look also for signs of sexual vitality—a deep, well-formed philtrum; slightly full, light undereye area; clear palaces of marriage and a glowing position point. (Yes, ask the other's age!)
- Be alert to signals of sexual promiscuity (see page 219).
- Look at the forehead for character and background.
- Look at the Parent Points (Points 17 and 18) as indicators of how this person was treated by his or her parents. If the person was treated well, he or she will probably be good to a mate and children.
- Look at the ears to discover what kind of child this person was, forecasting what kind of adult he or she has become, and also for wisdom, a spirit of adventure and the prospect of long life.
- The nose reveals much about the quality of family life as well as the prospects in career. For a good family life, the nose should be well formed at the root (Point 41) and at the bridge (points 44 and 45); and the Peak of Perfection (Point 48) should be well shaped and rounded to indicate financial well-being. The nostrils are best when they are slightly flared (not too tight to the nose) to indicate generosity.
- The mouth is best if it is large and slightly squared, to indicate a balanced and amiable personality.
- Look for long, curved laugh lines and other indicators of longevity.
- Look for a strong chin for strength and vitality in the later years.

NOTE: The partner with the stronger cheekbones will be the dominant partner in the relationship.

What a Woman Should Look for in a Husband

The best thing to find in a prospective mate is heart—inner glow—which transforms even the most ordinary face into something wonderful. But in the flush of infatuation, the charisma of the charmer may be mistakenly read as heart. So keep some other signs in mind when you make your choice.

The keys are indicators of sexual vitality and fertility, and an ability to make money, achieve a position in life and generosity and longevity:

- a long, deep philtrum flared at the bottom (sexual vitality)
- a well shaped nose with round tip (money, career, good family life)
- flared nostrils (generosity)
- well-shaped ears with long lobes (wisdom)
- bony forehead (character)
- strong jawbones (status)
- long, curved laugh lines (longevity)
- smoothness at outer corners of the eye (fidelity)
- slightly full undereye area (fertility)
- large, balanced mouth (amiability)
- slightly squared chin (strength)

Negative signs:

- many crinkles at the corners of the eyes (infidelity)
- flat philtrum (lack of sexual drive)
- narrow, pinched nostrils (stinginess)
- horizontal line across root of the nose (hard on wife)

What a Man Should Look for in a Wife

Again, heart—inner glow—is the chief factor in a happy marriage. But with it, a man should hope to find indicators of comfort, gentleness, fertility, high status and money sense:

- round cherry mouth (comfort—the mark of the perfect wife in Chinese tradition)
- light, clear, slightly full undereye area (fertility)
- luminous eyes (intelligence)
- smoothness at corners of the eyes (fidelity)

- medium-high, round forehead (amiability)
- smooth, glossy hair (docility)
- round-tip nose (money accumulation)

Negative factors to avoid:

- protruding eyes and a tendency to keep the mouth open (lack of modesty)
- very high, very square hairline (early widowhood)
- very strong cheekbones (domineering)
- long, pointed chin (gossip)
- oval chin (vain, weakness in old age)
- dark, sunken undereye area (low fertility)
- wide, flaring nostrils (extravagance)

GUIDELINES

Bear in mind that when we are choosing a mate, we often choose someone who "completes our self"—who has characteristics that complement our own or who compensates for our deficiencies. So, in choosing a life partner, first evaluate your own face and then decide what needs you have and what characteristics in the other will fill them.

4. OTHERS IN YOUR LIFE

We all need a variety of people in our lives, and these fulfill various roles—friends, family, companion, confidant, co-worker, guests, hosts, teammates and so on. Here are some of the indicators of what a person is like, as an aid for understanding associates better:

Pleasant people. Some people are just plain nice—pleasant to be around and wonderful as companions, co-workers and family members. Often, they don't display amazing talents, and they may not even aspire to great achievement, though most of them do well for themselves. Often, they become the most important people in our lives. Look for:

- small, round, well-shaped ears
- half-moon eyebrows or smooth, arched eyebrows
- ox eyes
- deer nose
- rounded jaw and chin
- soft, smooth hair
- inner glow

Hard-to-live-with people. Some people are hard to live with just because they tend to be domineering and want to run things. Often, though, they are interesting people, and you put up with them for the good qualities they also display. Be warned by:

- long, pointed chin
- thin, wide mouth
- cheekbones high and square with strong bone and base
- tiger eyes
- dark, heavy eyebrows
- square jaw
- eyes set far apart
- very angular hairline

Party people. Some people are fun to be around—natural socialites, they make wonderful guests, give great parties and liven up any get-together. Look for:

- crescent mouth
- willow eyebrows
- round, well-shaped ears with protruding inner rim
- ears with no lobe
- blue eyes
- peach-blossom hairline
- mole at the Society Point
- heart-shaped face

Lonely people. Some people like to be alone, are generally poor mixers and often appear lonely, although they are so by choice. Such a person may have deep-set eyes and a small mouth. There are, however, some people who are truly lonely, not by choice. If you are alone more than you like and have any of the following characteristics, you may want to change those features that can be changed.

- Skin is rough, like an orange peel.
- Many forehead lines.
- Ears thin, no definite wheels.
- Eyebrows shorter than eyes and very close to eyes.
- Undereye area is sunken and dark.
- Eyes are beady.
- Nose not strong or bridge is sunken.
- Tip of nose is pointed.
- Philtrum is flat.
- Lips have many crisscross lines.
- Mouth doesn't close properly.
- Face has sad expression.
- Voice is dry and tearful.
- Breathing pattern is tight.

Other traits to be aware of. Here are some of the characteristics you should become aware of when you form associations:

Jealous: upturned eyes; small eyes.
Miserly: monkey mouth; thin nose, thin pinched nostrils; nose with pointed tip; small ears that are tight to the head.
Enthusiastic: short nose; blue eyes; uptilted eyes.
Sensual: thick eyelids; thick ears.
Romantic: deep-set eyes.
Generous: nostrils full and flared.
Spendthrift: upturned nose; reddish nose; upswept eyebrows.
Gossip: matchmaker's mole.
Self-indulgent: tapering jaw; oval chin or cleft chin; fleshy ears.
Fierce: eyebrows joined; protruding chin; short lashes.
Misfit: hectic glitter in eyes; three-white-sided eye.
Charismatic: cat's eyes.

III

STAGING YOUR LIFE THROUGH FACE AND FEATURE READING

Staging your life through face reading is one benefit that can be very significant to you. Many people have a rather unrealistic idea of what life is going to deliver to them over the span of a lifetime—and thus fail to realize their potential, either by ignoring the possibilities as they and the conditions of their life change or by living only in the present, without considering how rewarding the future can be.

Through face reading, you can discover when to act to take greatest advantage of opportunities and when to coast or regroup your forces.

Staging applies equally to personal and family life and your career development.

In career, it is important to secure your fortune at each period of your working life for a comfortable and secure old age. In family life, though most men and women find it easy to pair up in youth, they must also evaluate the chances of a stable family life in the middle years and the prospects of having a life companion as well as children and grandchildren to comfort their later years and to share its rewards.

Throughout the life span, the prospects of maintaining good health are important to career and family well-being and strength in maturity.

Once you are aware of your prospects, the times you can take advantage of your strengths and when you need to roll with adversity, you have much more to look forward to and a more optimistic and confident view of things.

1. FINDING YOUR DIRECTION

Analyzing your elemental type tells you what direction and what field of employment will best be yours.

If you are predominantly Fire or have a strong Fire component, you will look for a colorful, adventurous life. Whatever field of work you enter, you will choose an aspect of it that has a strong element of showmanship—meeting the public, competing openly and so on. In your personal life, you will want action and consequently will move in interesting social circles.

If you are predominantly Water or have a strong Water component, you will look for a chance to make money, either by working in the financial field, through investments or by getting into a rewarding area of employment in whatever field you enter. In your personal life, you will want a great deal of flexibility and association with money centers of the world and will tend to associate with monied people.

If you are predominantly Wood or have a strong Wood component, you will be attracted to the thinking professions or the arts and sciences, where your innate intellectuality can have influence. In your personal and family life, you will strive for intellectual interests and cultural and creative opportunities.

If you are predominantly Earth or have a strong Earth component, you will be attracted by industry or any field of business where you are assured of security and stability. In your personal life, you will look for stabilizing factors and the chance to establish yourself in one place, and will want a stable social background.

If you are predominantly Gold or have a strong Gold component, you will be attracted to management positions where you can rise in status and achieve high rank. In personal life, you will look for balance and grace and the chance to associate with the elite of your community.

How Will Your Energies Be Directed?

Analyze your cosmic energies to see where your energies will be best directed. To the Yang—active, working side of life—or to the Yin—cultural, emotional, family side of life—or will you maintain a balance?

Many women are attracted to the Yin—home and family—by choice as well as by tradition, while others are basically Yang-directed and want a lifetime career as well as home and family. Men, in our tradition, are basically required to develop the Yang energies in order to make a living. However, every field of work has its active Yang and its receptive Yin side. We are all made up of Yin and Yang, but in some, the Yang energy is dominant (boniness), and in others, the Yin energy dominates (fleshy, soft). In others, the balance is apparent.

When Will Your Energies Be Most Effective?

The Three Stations reveal the part of life—youth, middle years, old age—when your chances of success will be greatest. Possibly all three stations are balanced, and this gives you an effective life plan. Others have their greatest chance for success in their youth (First Station), others in middle life (Second Station) and still others receive their fruits in the later period (Third Station). If you are an early bloomer, your greatest achievement comes before age thirty. If you have a dominant middle station, you may have to defer success until the stable middle period—a period that also stabilizes family life. If your Third Station is dominant, you make your move late in life.

What Are Your Potentials for Achievement?

Whatever your direction, the dominant form of your energy and the part of life when you can expect to achieve most, you need to know your potential for achievement in whatever area you enter. This is shown in the Five Major Features. The limitation or range of this potential is modified by the Seven

Minor Features, and you will be further helped or hindered by the lesser features—hair, facial lines and so on.

Look, too, at your longevity factors—good health and long life are vital to the full use of your potential.

What Is Your Approach?

Your voice and your posture—how you hold your head—have much to do with projecting the image of vitality and the ability to sustain your potentiality. The voice is best if it is strong and deep, like a bell, indicating strong lungs and heart as well as confidence. The face itself is Yang—the Sun—and lights up the world around you. Holding the face down or letting the head droop interferes with your light and can be a handicap.

Do You Have Warmth, Inner Glow?

This, as you know, is the sign of inner balance and a chance to star.

2. PLOTTING YOUR COURSE

Progress in work and family life is mapped out for you on your face in a number of ways.

The position points. As your floating year moves through the various position points, you progress through the experiences of the various positions in the court, indicative of the events and kind of success you can have at each point. It is a good idea to look backward and forward at the meaning of these positions to see what is in store in the immediate future and what you should have gained in the recent past. This way you can plot your progress from year to year.

The planetary periods. The influence of particular planets over various periods of life is another tool, an indicator of the kind of energy you will be applying to life at each stage.

- From conception through age 13, you are under the influence of Venus (Gold Star) and Jupiter (Wood Star). These are the periods of early growth and development.

- From age 14 through 30, you are in the Mars period, when the adventurous vitality of Fire shapes your activities.
- In your thirties, you are in the star-point period. This is the time when the creative Yang and Yin energies help you shine.
- From age 40, you are in the Saturn (Earth Star) period—a period of achievement and stabilization of family life, when the security of Earth dominates your approach. You reach a peak at age 48, with a new start of productivity beginning at age 50.
- From age 60, you are in the Mercury (Water Star) phase— a time when you enjoy the richness of maturity and the fruits of your life, including children and grandchildren as well as material wealth. This is a time when flexibility dominates your activities.

The Thirteen Middle Points. The high spots of the position points and the influence of the planets are tied together in a reading of the Thirteen Middle Points. These show the stepping stones through the Column of Heaven to the Root of the Mountain and thence to the Peak of Perfection and on to the Sea of Wine and at last Buried Treasure. These Middle Points reveal the appropriate actions and experiences at the major highpoints of your life and let you stage your progress accordingly.

Day-to-day checkup. In addition to the condition of your current position point, the appropriate palace should be checked for the prospects of a fortunate outcome for any enterprise you are currently engaged in. For some of the special events of life, more than one area should be consulted:

Travel: Check the Stagecoaches (the Palaces of Transfer) and also check the Sea of Wine, the area below the lower lip, for prospects in travel. Also consult the appropriate month in the Calendar of the Face (pages 233–235).

Romance: Check the Palaces of Marriage and also the Sleeping Silkworm (undereye area) and the philtrum (the groove from the nostrils to the upper lip) and the star points.

Money: Consult the Palace of Wealth (the tip of the nose) and also the Palaces of Happiness and Good Fortune.

Success: Check the Palace of Achievement (mid forehead) and also the star points and your current position point.

Health: Check the Palace of Health (root of the nose) and also the appropriate color of the planet points and your current position point.

IV

YOUR FACE AND YOUR HEALTH

As we have seen, the face lets you make a quick check of your health by comparing the various features with the appropriate planetary color:

- ears—pinkish white, lighter than the face
- forehead—pink and glowing
- eyes—clear and luminous
- nose—golden tan and shiny
- mouth—rosy red

You can also check your vitality by examining your current position point. When it appears warm and glowing, you are probably up to par in vitality.

The features also are related to various body organs and reflect inner health by color or appearance, according to the ancient Chinese.

- The ears represent the kidneys and should be neither too dry nor too red for good health. Discoloration, grayness or greenish color indicate poor function.

- The eyes represent the liver. Yellowish color in the white of the eye is a warning color. Redness or lack of glow is also a danger signal.
- The nose represents the lungs as well as the male sex organ. The appropriate color is golden tan. Too red, too pale or too grayish or greenish is an indicator of respiratory disorder as well as diminished stamina.
- The mouth represents the female sex organ, but the lips also represent the spleen. The appropriate color is rosy red. The lips should be neither too moist nor too dry, neither too pale nor too dark, for optimum condition.

1. THE CALENDAR OF THE FACE

The Chinese art of face reading also provides a monthly checkup on health and other fortunes through the calendar of the face (following page). Look at the current month and then check the appropriate area (position points) of the face for its color. This will tell you the fortune this month might bring.

THE CALENDAR OF THE FACE

Month	Area of Face	Fortunate Color(s) and Meaning	Other Colors and Meaning
January	right jaw Points 80-81	clear and whitish—good luck purplish—money coming in	reddish—fire hazards gray green—robbery alert
February	right cheek Points 82-83	golden, pinkish, light purple—fortunate purplish red—brings money	too white, too dark—accident hazard yellowish brown—fights
March	right temple Points 84-85	pink—happy events, love affairs, marriage, a trip home golden—promotion	cloudy—problems white—health disorders, accidents
April	right sides of forehead Points 86-87	light pink—travel, promotion light purple—money	too white or dark—family problems tawny, yellowish—ventures may not succeed
May	mid-forehead Points 88-89	purple—high position pinkish—romance golden—unexpected good luck	white—danger from water dusky—fire hazards
June	left side of forehead Points 90-91	pinkish—success in an important enterprise purplish—money within a month golden—success	white or dusky (grayish)—problems

234

Month	Location		
July	left temple Points 92-93	golden and clear—romance, children	dark—danger of misfortune reddish—accident hazards white—chance of illness purplish—routine period
August	left side of cheek Points 94-95	golden yellow—smooth going white—average fortune	very red—unfortunate; likely to have problems, warning of natural disasters dark—danger of misfortunes
September	left jaw Points 96-97	clear—good fortune	cloudy—chance of bad luck redness—chance of illness yellow—liver and gall bladder complaints (biliousness)
October	left lower jaw Points 98-99	shiny, bright—good times, money, happy events purplish—smooth but no great fortune	red—fire hazards yellowish white—chance of illness
November	chin Points 76-77	purplish, glowing—very lucky	red, cloudy—accident hazards all other colors indicate an average condition
December	right lower jaw Points 78-79	ivory—fortunate	all other colors are not fortunate

2. WILL COSMETIC SURGERY CHANGE YOUR FORTUNE?

The ancient Chinese, of course, did not practice cosmetic surgery, so anything said here is speculative. We know that the Chinese believed that heart—inner glow—could transform negative features into a positive effect. We also know that poor habits of health and life-style can change the face and turn positive features into negative ones—in depression, for example, the mouth may droop and the eyes lose their glow. Loss of teeth or bone can alter the mouth and chin. Poor health habits can change the planetary colors.

We also know that a positive attitude toward one's appearance can improve inner glow and so improve one's fortune. So if cosmetic surgery has a positive effect on the personality, it may certainly be a benefit for one's present fortune, if not one's fate.

The most common cosmetic surgeries involve the eyes, the nose and various lifts to firm the lower part of the face. Eye surgery affects the palaces both of Marriage and of Offspring. However, in women, it is usually done after the childbearing years. In a youth-oriented society, it may improve chances for a late marriage for women. In men, it serves mainly as a youth restorer—but it also eliminates signs of promiscuity (crinkles at the corners of the eyes). In this way, it may indeed improve your fate.

Nose remodeling usually serves to turn a fat or high-bridged nose into a thinner, bonier nose. As people tend to "follow their nose"—that is, be like their nose—it is possible that a more arrogant form to the nose may make the person more arrogant and self-centered. This may reduce their good fortune. However, the chief problem with surgical nose changes is that it makes it difficult to read the face correctly.

"Lifts" raise the laugh lines as well as the lower part of the face (jowls). Important here is that the location of the position points remains the same even after a lift.

Surgery to improve a receding chin often involves dental work and sometimes improves chewing (nutrition) and breathing, and this can only have a positive effect for strength in later years and can also improve status (jaws) by making one feel more acceptable to others. Here, again, your fortune may be changed for the better.

GUIDELINES

Anything that improves inner glow improves your fortune.

V

HELPING OTHERS THROUGH FACE READING

Besides using face reading to help yourself and to understand others better, you can use it to help other people. Many individuals do not appreciate their own good points or do not understand their true potential. And sometimes people simply feel they have nothing to look forward to. On other occasions, you will find that people are unaware of a diminishing vitality or a need to regenerate their cosmic energy.

Of course, much of your help may have to be given indirectly. You have to be tactful in imparting information, and you will not want to offer unwanted advice. Nor will you want to introduce negative thinking into a situation that may already be critical.

Realize at the start that everyone has at least one good feature, and that gives them ten happy years. Moreover, the development of inner glow transforms even negative features into a positive effect.

Emphasize the positive. Many people do not recognize their own good features, and often, if they do, do not know what the potential of that feature may be.

Often, simply calling attention to one good feature introduces a positive attitude. For example, if a person has strong eyebrows and a potential for fame and this is pointed out, the person may be motivated to put forth a greater effort in whatever he or she is doing. Or the promise of a high forehead for youthful success or the suggestion that a Peach blossom is not a widow's peak but the sign of a belle may lift another's spirits.

If someone complains about a negative beauty feature—for example, a wide mouth—she may be happy to be told that it is a Tiger Mouth and promises good fortune. Or if someone feels that his nose is too fat, the news that it is a nose for money is reassuring.

Even a somewhat negative feature can be given a positive slant—light, wispy eyebrows indicate a "man who makes a hit with women"; flaring nostrils—"you are very generous"; thin lips—"very determined." And so on.

Share promise of the future. One good way to help others through face reading is to give them a promise for the future. At some time, everyone has down periods. But it may brighten another's outlook considerably to know that his or her floating year is about to move to a position point that holds a promise of success, adventure, travel or marriage. This is particularly meaningful to those who are at a transition point into a new decade—especially entering the thirties, but even the twenties and, of course, the forties and fifties. You can deliver the good news: You are about to enter the star-point period (age 30). You are at the root of the mountain on the way to the peak (age 40). It's your sexual high point (age 50). Now you're floating on the Sea of Wine (age 60). People are often dismayed by these bridges, and a new way of looking forward instead of backward can be cheering and can bolster confidence.

When a person is about to embark on a particular enterprise, you can check the appropriate palace and give an encouraging word if the auspices are good or, if the prospects are disappointing, you can help the person over any discouragement by suggesting that if it doesn't work this time, there'll still be other chances. This may help ease the disappointment.

Help others in a better direction. Face reading also reveals limitations, helping you, perhaps, guide others out of blind alleys and hapless endeavors. Many people become misdirected in life, striving toward things they cannot attain, simply because they have never been given any guideline. Often, such people can reach higher goals in a more rewarding field if they have the courage to change. Again, it is necessary to be tactful and to point out the better direction, as indicated by their potentials, rather than to take a defeatist attitude toward whatever they are presently attempting. It may also be helpful to suggest that a person allow more time to achieve what he or she is after if the floating year or other indicator suggests that success will be further in the future than the individual feels it should be.

Check another's vitality. You can help another maintain vitality by checking the appropriate color of the features in relation to the planetary guidelines and subtly suggest a change of some kind— a day off from work, a vacation, a good night's sleep or a dietary change, even a physical checkup—if you think the vitality is low or if the person seems to be overdoing some task. The Calendar of the Face (see pages 233–235) is another method of keeping watch on someone's well-being. And if you know another's age, you can keep an eye on the position point to be sure it has glow and good color. If not, you might suggest a rest or change of pace to bring the cosmic energies back into balance.

Nurture another's inner glow. One of the better ways to help others through face reading is by nurturing their inner glow. This comes about through your own understanding of their potentials and limitations. The better you read people, the more tolerant you become of their foibles (and your own), and the more realistic your expectations of others can become. When you can truly appreciate the various assets and limitations that make up another's life potential, you get closer to the person's heart, and the inner glow can better express itself.

APPENDIXES

APPENDIX A—THE ELEMENTS

	Fire	Water	Earth	Gold	Wood
Planet	Mars	Mercury	Saturn	Venus	Jupiter
Color	Red	Black	Brown	White	Green
Helper	Wood	Gold	Fire	Earth	Water
Helps	Earth	Wood	Gold	Water	Fire
Hinders	Gold	Fire	Water	Wood	Earth
Hindering	Water	Earth	Wood	Fire	Gold
Vitality	Activity	Flexibility	Stillness	Grace	Rising
Fortune	Adventure	Wealth	Security	Status	Wisdom

APPENDIX B—THE ELEMENTAL TYPES

	Fire	Water	Earth	Gold	Wood
Face Shape	Conic	Round	Square	Oblong	Triangle
Complexion	Ruddy	Swarthy	Tawny	Ivory	Olive
Personality					
Positive	Outgoing	Adaptable	Practical	Diplomatic	Idealistic
Negative	Restless	Opportunistic	Aggressive	Dilettante	Unrealistic
Vocation	Show Business	Business, Finance	Industry	Management	Arts, Sciences
Combinations					
Harmonious	Wood, Earth	Gold, Wood	Fire, Gold	Earth, Water	Water, Fire
Inharmonious	Gold, Water	Fire, Earth	Water, Wood	Water, Fire	Earth, Gold

APPENDIX C—THE 100 POSITION POINTS

Point	Name	Personal Attribute	Destiny
1, 2	Upper Wheel of Heaven	wonder	growth
3, 4	Middle Wheel of Heaven	development	individualization
5, 6, 7	Pearl Drop of Heaven	knowledge	integration
8, 9	Upper Wheel of Humanity	creativity	exploration
10, 11	Middle Wheel of Humanity	belonging	choices
12, 13, 14	Pearl Drop of Humanity	idealism	conditioning
15	Mars	enthusiasm	initiation
16	Middle Sky	search	finding of identity
17	Sun Point	vigor	responsibility
18	Moon Point	compassion	approval
19	Court of Heaven	flowering	social acceptance
20	The Deputy	serving	experience
21	The Assistant	following	obedience
22	Steward of Heaven	capability	independence
23	The Fringe	adventure	movement
24	The Outskirts	experiment	change
25	Center of Heaven	influence	triumph
26	The Monument	brightness	a turning point
27	The Mausoleum	reflection	inheritance
28	The Shrine of the Seal of Heaven	daring	good fortune
29	Mountain or Highland	moving upward	expression

Point	Name	Personal Attribute	Destiny
	APPENDIX C, continued		
30	The Forest	wandering	transition
31	Floating Cloud	confidence	recognition
32	Purple Air	enjoyment	satisfaction
33	Colorful Rainbow	discernment	opportunity
34	Kaleidoscope of Color	selectivity	adjustment
35	Yang	inner energy	affirmation
36	Yin	inner strength	receptivity
37	Middle Yang	resoluteness	progress
38	Middle Yin	intuition	unfolding
39L	Late Yang	awareness	increase
40	Late Yin	enlightenment	fulfillment
41	The Root of the Mountain	family reunion	holding together
42	Delicate Cottage	intimacy	introspection
43	Bright Palace	conviviality	self-expression
44	Sitting on Top of One's Age	stamina	vitality
45	Sitting on Top of One's Longevity	resourcefulness	accumulation
46	The Summit	authority	power over others
47	The Crest	resistance	power over oneself
48	Peak of Perfection	self-satisfaction	success
49	The Balcony	looking ahead	public service
50	The Pagoda	militance	acclaim
51	Center of Life	sexuality	productivity
52	Warehouse	pride	acquisitiveness

Point	Name	Personal Attribute	Destiny
53	Storage Area	evaluation	merchandising
54	Food Depot	nourishment	providence
55	Strong Room	vigilance	protection
56	Law	optimism	justice
57	Order	compliance	regulation
58	The Guardian	alertness	guardianship
59	The Defender	bravado	trophies
60	Mercury—The Water of Life	indulgence	trust
61	Sea of Wine	enjoyment	travel
62, 63	Cellars and Basements	precaution	support
64-65	Pools of Water	contemplation	serenity
66-67	Golden Robes	well-being	honors
68-69	Return	sociability	entertainment
70	Court of Justice	balance	judgment
71	Buried Treasure	understanding	riches
72, 73	Servants and Helpers	dependency	management
74, 75	Status	remembrance	veneration
76-77	The Rat	cleverness	hope
78-79	The Ox	patience	duration
80-81	The Tiger	thought	victory
82-83	The Hare	gentleness	friends
84-85	The Dragon	pleasure	rulership
86-87	The Snake	charisma	higher mind
88-89	The Horse	diplomacy	display
90-91	The Ram	flexibility	breakthrough
92-93	The Monkey	curiosity	dominance
94-95	The Cock	sophistication	perspective
96-97	The Dog	loyalty	truth
98-99	The Boar	self-will	leadership
100	Completion		

APPENDIX D—THE ANIMAL SYMBOL
FOR THE YEAR OF YOUR BIRTH

On the next two pages are the Animal Symbols for the years 1900 to 1995. Notice the dates in parentheses; they represent the date on which the Chinese New Year begins (unlike our New Year, which falls on January 1, the Chinese New Year varies from year to year).

To find your animal symbol, first locate the year in which you were born. Then:

If you were born *on or after* the date in parentheses, simply match your birth year with the corresponding symbol. For example, a person born on April 25, 1954, was born in the Year of the Horse.

If you were born between January 1 and the date in parentheses (that is, *before* the date in parentheses), look at the year preceding your birth year and match that with the corresponding symbol. For example, a person born on February 17, 1958, was born in the Year of the Cock, not the Year of the Dog.

Rat	Ox	Tiger	Rabbit	Dragon	Snake
1900 (1/31)*	1901 (2/18)	1902 (2/8)	1903 (1/29)	1904 (2/16)	1905 (2/4)
1912 (2/18)	1913 (2/6)	1914 (1/26)	1915 (2/14)	1916 (2/3)	1917 (1/23)
1924 (2/5)	1925 (1/25)	1926 (2/13)	1927 (2/2)	1928 (1/23)	1929 (2/10)
1936 (1/24)	1937 (2/11)	1938 (1/31)	1939 (2/19)	1940 (2/8)	1941 (1/27)
1948 (2/10)	1949 (1/29)	1950 (2/17)	1951 (2/6)	1952 (1/27)	1953 (2/14)
1960 (1/28)	1961 (2/15)	1962 (2/5)	1963 (1/25)	1964 (2/13)	1965 (2/2)
1972 (2/15)	1973 (2/3)	1974 (1/23)	1975 (2/11)	1976 (1/31)	1977 (2/18)
1984 (2/2)	1985 (2/20)	1986 (2/9)	1987 (1/29)	1988 (2/17)	1989 (2/6)

*with starting date of the Chinese New Year

Horse	Sheep	Monkey	Cock	Dog	Boar
1906 (1/25)	1907 (2/13)	1908 (2/2)	1909 (1/22)	1910 (2/10)	1911 (1/30)
1918 (2/11)	1919 (2/1)	1920 (2/20)	1921 (2/8)	1922 (1/28)	1923 (2/16)
1930 (1/30)	1931 (2/17)	1932 (2/6)	1933 (1/26)	1934 (2/14)	1935 (2/4)
1942 (2/15)	1943 (2/5)	1944 (1/25)	1945 (2/13)	1946 (2/2)	1947 (1/22)
1954 (2/3)	1955 (1/24)	1956 (2/12)	1957 (1/31)	1958 (2/18)	1959 (2/8)
1966 (1/21)	1967 (2/9)	1968 (1/30)	1969 (2/17)	1970 (2/6)	1971 (1/27)
1978 (2/7)	1979 (1/28)	1980 (2/16)	1981 (1/25)	1982 (2/13)	1983 (2/13)
1990 (1/27)	1991 (2/15)	1992 (2/4)	1993 (1/23)	1994 (2/10)	1995 (1/31)

APPENDIX E—THE FACE AS A CLOCK

The chart that follows lets you discover the time of day that may prove fortuitous for your various enterprises. First, find the animal symbol for the year of your birth (see appendix D). Then, read across the line to the column on the extreme right to locate the hours most favorable for you. Do the same with your astrological sign. (Note that you can have *two* fortunate time periods.) The position point column on the extreme right shows the points on the perimeter of the face that represent particular hours of the day. When these points are warm and glowing, the hours are superfortunate.

Position Point	Animal Symbol	Astrological Sign	Hour of Day or Night
76, 77 (100)	Rat	Aries	11 P.M.– 1 A.M.
78, 79	Ox	Taurus	1 A.M.– 3 A.M.
80, 81	Tiger	Gemini	3 A.M.– 5 A.M.
82, 83	Hare	Cancer	5 A.M.– 7 A.M.
84, 85	Dragon	Leo	7 A.M.– 9 A.M.
86, 87	Snake	Virgo	9 A.M.–11 A.M.
88, 89	Horse	Libra	11 A.M.– 1 P.M.
90, 91	Goat	Scorpio	1 P.M.– 3 P.M.
92, 93	Monkey	Sagittarius	3 P.M.– 5 P.M.
94, 95	Cock	Capricorn	5 P.M.– 7 P.M.
96, 97	Dog	Aquarius	7 P.M.– 9 P.M.
98, 99	Boar	Pisces	9 P.M.–11 P.M.

About the Authors

PETER SHEN is currently creative director for Aziza Cosmetics and Prince Matchabelli Perfumes and has created the faces of many famous models and celebrities. Born on his grandfather's ancestral estate in Shanghai, he moved to Australia, then Tokyo, where he studied at the International Christian University and the Tokyo Art School. Because he was born on July Fourth and shared the United States' birthday, Mr. Shen decided to come to the United States, where he worked as an actor and did layout and art work for advertising agencies. Through his work in advertising, he became involved in Estée Lauder's Aramis line and traveled for them, setting up major promotional and publicity campaigns. In 1970, Mr. Shen was asked to develop a cosmetic line for Aziza and has since been with that company. He is also the author of *Peter Shen's Makeup for Success*.

JOYCE WILSON is the author of over a dozen books including *The Complete Book of Palmistry* and is the co-author of *Peter Shen's Makeup for Success*. She lives in New York City.